A MODEL OF CORRECTIONAL LEADERSHIP: THE CAREER OF NORMAN A. CARLSON

By

Clemens Bartollas, Ph.D.

To Scott Pustizzi,
Warm regards,
Norm Carlson

Mission of the American Correctional Association
American Correctional Association provides a professional organization for all individuals and groups, both public and private, that share a common goal of improving the justice system.

American Correctional Association Staff
Harold W. Clarke, President
James A. Gondles, Jr., C.A.E., Executive Director
Gabriella M. Klatt, Director, Communications and Publications
Alice Heiserman, Manager, Publications and Research
Jeannelle Ferreira, Associate Editor
Ryan Bounds, Intern
Leigh Ann Bright, Graphics and Production Associate
Cover design by Xavaire Bolton

Copyright 2010 by the American Correctional Association. All rights reserved. The reproduction, distribution, or inclusion in other publications of materials in this book is prohibited without prior written permission from the American Correctional Association. No part of this book may be reproduced by any electronic means including information storage and retrieval systems without permission in writing from the publisher. Printed in the United States of America by Gasch Printing, Odenton, Md.

ISBN 978-1-56991-322-2

This publication may be ordered from:
American Correctional Association
206 N. Washington St., Suite 200
Alexandria, Virginia 22314
800-222-5646 ext. 0129

For information on publications and videos available from ACA, contact our worldwide web home page at: www.aca.org

Library of Congress Cataloging-in-Publication Data
Bartollas, Clemens.
A model of correctional leadership: the career of Norman A. Carlson/by Clemens Bartollas. — 1st ed.
p. cm.
Includes bibliographical references and index.
ISBN 978-1-56991-322-2
1. Carlson, Norman A., 1933- 2. Correctional personnel—United States—Biography. I. Title.
HV9468.C367B37 2010
365'.92--dc22   [B]   2010002099

Table of Contents

Foreword by Harley Lappin, Director,
Federal Bureau of Prisons v
Foreword by James A. Gondles, Jr., CAE ix
Dedication xi
Preface xiii

Chapter 1. INTRODUCTION 1

PART I   PERSONAL HISTORY 11
    Chapter 2.   Life Before the Bureau of Prisons 12
    Chapter 3.   Fast Rise to the Top: 1957-1969 23
    Chapter 4.   The Buck Stops Here: The Turbulent 1970s 39
    Chapter 5.   Leadership in the 1980s 63
    Chapter 6.   Post-Retirement Years 75

**PART II   OUTSTANDING LEADERSHIP AND
PARADIGM SHIFTS** 87
    Chapter 7.   Personal Attributes and
                  Outstanding Leadership 89
    Chapter 8.   Management and Principles of Leadership 109
    Chapter 9.   Innovations and Change 127
    Chapter 10.   Ripples of Norman Carlson's Leadership 149
    Chapter 11.   From a Good to a Great Organization 177

**PART III   NORMAN CARLSON'S CONTRIBUTIONS TO
THE PRESENT** 187
    Chapter 12.   Norman Carlson's Influence
                  on Corrections 189
    Chapter 13.   Norman Carlson's Other Contributions
                  to Corrections 203
    Chapter 14.   Summary 209

Index 217
About the Author 233

Foreword

By Harley Lappin, Director, Federal Bureau of Prisons

The twenty-first century Federal Bureau of Prisons owes much to the leadership, wisdom, and vision of Norman A. Carlson, its fourth director. Director Carlson is best remembered for moving the Bureau of Prisons into the modern age, improving upon and adapting some of the principles of the three prior directors into a program of excellence that has withstood the test of time and phenomenal growth. Today, the Bureau of Prisons operates 115 correctional facilities and has contracts with 14 privately operated secure facilities and hundreds of community-based facilities and local jails. It has an inmate population of more than 210,000 inmates and approximately 37,000 staff members. When Director Carlson left the Bureau, there were 44,000 inmates in 47 federal correctional institutions, with a staff complement of nearly 13,000.

Director Carlson accepted the mantle of Director in March 1970 after serving as Director Myrl E. Alexander's executive assistant for four years. He began his career with the Bureau in 1957, working first as a parole officer at the United States Penitentiary in Leavenworth, Kansas. He worked at the Federal Correctional Institution in Ashland, Kentucky, prior to coming to the Bureau's Central Office in 1960, where he served for one year as the assistant supervisor of the Institutional Programs Division. Just prior to working for Director Alexander, Carlson spent four years directing the development of a Community Treatment Center program for the Bureau. In 1965, he was selected to participate in the Woodrow Wilson School of Public and International Affairs at Princeton University.

Carlson rose quickly through the ranks of the Bureau as a result of the creativity and initiative he displayed in every assignment he received. He was a masterful communicator, readily translating his ideas into practical solutions that had widespread appeal and netted positive results. Many administrators enjoy the art of creative thinking, but few have the wherewithal to put those ideas into practice; not so with Carlson. When he had an idea about some creative way of improving operations at the Bureau, he saw that idea through to fruition and implementation in Bureau policy and/or practice. Director Carlson understood early the importance of computers in prison management and the value of research to identify initiatives that produced positive results.

Director Carlson's vision of where the agency should go and what it should be doing can be seen in countless areas of the Bureau's work. The agency's mission statement and core values stem directly from principles he espoused. He not only recognized the importance of professionalism and integrity in the work we do, but he emphasized the need for respect for our associates and the inmates we serve. Bureau employees, today, are proud to be part of a close-knit family; something Director Carlson promoted during his tenure.

His tenure as Director left other important legacies that have been expanded and refined over time. The most obvious include unit management, inmate classification, professionalism, safety, and research. Although initiated under the Myrl Alexander directorship in the youth facility in Morgantown, West Virginia, the broader use of the unit management concept in adult institutions occurred during Norm Carlson's tenure. Unit management decentralized the focus of correctional work, allowing for more individualized attention for each offender. It allowed for much more interaction between staff and inmates and reduced the bureaucratic structure by arranging facilities into small units, each with its own staff and each supervised by its own unit manager. The current agency focus on inmate skills development (see discussion below) was a natural outgrowth of this individualized focus.

The principles of inmate classification developed under Director Carlson's leadership include: 1) safety for inmates, staff, and communities; 2) consistency and fairness to inmates; and 3) cost efficiencies. By classifying inmates correctly, like inmates can be housed together and appropriate security measures taken, protecting not only inmates and staff, but society as well. The same is true for cost efficiencies; low security inmates do not require more costly security measures, such as individual cells and restricted movement.

He stressed the importance of professionalism among staff members, providing them with enhanced training programs, including Introduction to Correctional Techniques for all new staff members, and a variety of courses in management, supervision, and discipline-specific skills for in-service staff. He encouraged professionalism through attire and language, discouraging rough language and changing their titles from "guards" to "correctional officers." He emphasized the importance of effective communication with inmates and staff's responsibility as role models for inmates, exemplifying behavior indicative of a law-abiding lifestyle.

Director Carlson recognized that an effective inmate classification system had to be validated; thus, reinforcing an appreciation for the value of research. Director Carlson developed a strong research group within the Bureau with highly qualified staff expected to conduct independent evaluations of Bureau programs; a practice that continues today.

Rehabilitation has fallen in and out of favor as a goal of correctional confinement. Despite a widespread discrediting of the medical model in criminology, Director Carlson never lost sight of the importance of inmate programs, recognizing that offenders had very little chance of succeeding in the outside world if they did not learn new skills that would help them avoid the road back to criminal behavior. His emphasis on teaching

> **FBOP CORE VALUES**
>
> **CORRECTIONAL EXCELLENCE:** We are correctional workers first, committed to the highest level of performance.
>
> **RESPECT:** We embrace diversity and recognize the value and dignity of staff, inmates, and the general public.
>
> **INTEGRITY:** We demonstrate uncompromising ethical conduct in all our actions.

inmate skills remains strong within the Bureau today, and is epitomized in the latter portion of our Mission Statement: "... provide work and other self-improvement opportunities to assist offenders in becoming law-abiding citizens." In today's parlance, rehabilitation is known as "reentry," with renewed awareness within correctional systems and the general public that offenders eventually will return to their local communities.

Many of today's inmate programs owe their genesis to Norm Carlson, and are in keeping with the principles of all the previous Bureau of Prisons' directors. The mindset for always seeking improvement, whether in inmate programs, institutions, or staff professionalism, reflects back on the creative insights developed under Director Carlson.

Although Director Carlson did not anticipate (nor did anyone else) the rapid and unprecedented growth in the federal prison population, the principles and programs he established have served the agency very well through the significant expansion. Norm Carlson will long be remembered for his creativity, leadership, and foresight; and for these and other important improvements, we thank Director Carlson for all his efforts on behalf of this agency.

FEDERAL BUREAU OF PRISONS' MISSION STATEMENT

The Federal Bureau of Prisons protects society by confining offenders in the controlled environment of prisons and community-based facilities that are safe, humane, cost-efficient, and appropriately secure, and that provide work and other self-improvement opportunities to assist offenders in becoming law-abiding citizens.

Foreword

By James A. Gondles, Jr., CAE
Executive Director, American Correctional Association

We are proud to be publishing the only authorized biography of one of the legends in American corrections, Norman A. Carlson. Norm Carlson has a long history with the American Correctional Association. He was active in ACA for many years before he was president (1978-1980) and remains active on the Past Presidents' Council. Norm was instrumental in developing ACA standards and promoting their adoption nationally for the operation of correctional facilities and programs.

Norm is a tangible reminder of great leadership. Those who know him will be interested in the details of his career. Those who did not have the honor of working with him will find his story inspirational and the lessons of his principles educational.

As Clemens Bartollas clearly states:

> Norman Carlson is a further reminder of those who are considering corrections as a career or who are early in their corrections careers of what it is possible for them to accomplish. Ultimately, Norman Carlson's life and leadership is a reminder that humans can be more than they usually are, that there is far more to human potential then we can see in our clearest moments, and that humans joined together with others of kindred minds and spirits can transform the earth.

All around us we have reminders of the things Norm Carlson started. As ACA members and other corrections professionals come together at each year at our Congress of Correction and Winter Conference, we see many of our current correctional leaders who were given their training and support under Carlson's direction. The list of these individuals is long and impressive. I am personally proud to know Norm Carlson and to have witnessed his influence, ideas, opinions, leadership, and friendship.

Dedication

The late Pat Sledge, a long-time employee of the Federal Bureau of Prisons, was extremely helpful in the writing of this biography. She loved the Federal Bureau of Prisons and considered it part of her family.

In many ways, Pat, an African-American woman, personifies the men and women who have made their career at the Bureau. She began as a part-time employee during the early 1970s under a program designed to encourage high school students in Washington, D.C. to stay in school. She did very well in that assignment and, as a result, was given a permanent entry-level position when she graduated.

Pat was outstanding in all her subsequent assignments in the Central Office and was encouraged by her supervisors to transfer to a correctional institution for additional experience. She took that advice and accepted a position at the Federal Medical Center in Springfield, Missouri. She later was promoted to a unit manager's position at the Federal Correctional Institution in Morgantown, West Virginia. She was Director Carlson's executive assistant from 1981 until he retired in 1987. She subsequently served as the Bureau's site acquisition coordinator for all institutions and was then promoted to become deputy assistant director, the position she held when she retired (not a bad career for a potential high school dropout).

John Clark, a retired assistant director of the Bureau, spoke at Pat Sledge's funeral in 2006. Here is part of the eulogy he delivered:

> Pat Sledge. What a class act! What a warm, vibrant, and talented woman. BOP folks I have talked with the past few days have used so many similar adjectives and told so many stories. People are telling Pat Sledge stories with a big smile on their faces, remembering this woman who combined a savvy toughness with elegance, and who brought to the Bureau, a great organization—but, let's face it, a rather stodgy

federal correctional agency—a bit of big city splash and sass.

Later in the eulogy Clark continues:

I soon learned that she was the director's designated problem solver—especially with the most sensitive, sticky Washington-type problems—be it with a difficult committee of federal judges, an aggressive defense lawyer, or her specialty—the know-it-all congressional aide. Director Carlson simply said, 'Pat handle it.' And she did. She could be forceful and direct but also had an innate sense of diplomacy. What a touch she had!

To this remarkable woman, who contributed so much to the Federal Bureau of Prisons and who aided me so much in writing Norm Carlson's biography, I am pleased to dedicate this work.

Preface

I have been on quite a journey—an opportunity to research and write the biography of Norman A. Carlson, director of the Federal Bureau of Prisons from 1970-1987. Norman Carlson offers a fascinating story of a man who was an outstanding leader of a major government agency. My wife would repeatedly tell me, "I have never seen you so excited about writing anything" and after authoring forty books, that is quite a compliment to the legacy of the subject of this book.

The biography arose from my thinking that Norman Carlson was an exemplary leader of the Federal Bureau of Prisons during the 1970s and 1980s, decades that were troubling and challenging for American corrections. I decided to approach him about my doing a biography of his life. I did this, and he agreed.

Fortunately, he had read the biography that I had done on Frank Wood, (*Becoming a Model Warden: Striving for Excellence*, published by the American Correctional Association). Wood was a prison warden and later Commissioner of Corrections in Minnesota, and Carlson liked this biography. This perhaps contributed to his receptiveness. Nevertheless, his agreement to the biography did puzzle many folks who had worked with him in the Bureau. Several questioned me when I asked them for interviews, "How did you talk Norm into this?"

Carlson's biography was inspiring in many ways. The motivation certainly came from the interviews I conducted over the phone, the e-mails, and the letters I received on Norman Carlson. Nearly every one of the eighty interviewees, in one way or the other, reported the same message—it was a honor to work for and with this individual; he was a remarkable human being, an amazing leader, and a great man. The inspiration also came from my interviews with Norm and from his continued patience as I raised question after question on his life and career. The inspiration increased when I read about Norm and his career in the Bureau of Prisons, as well as his life since his retirement from the Bureau. While reporting on the career of this highly respected public servant, I was able to identify the paradigm shifts that resulted from Carlson's leadership during his thirty-year career with the Federal Bureau of Prisons.

I hope that the inspiration I felt will be transmitted to the readers of this biography and enable them to emulate the qualities that made Norman Carlson such an excellent leader and individual. The following summarized statements from people who worked with Carlson illustrate his legacy.

- Norman A. Carlson continued a culture of excellence in the Federal Bureau of Prisons during the seventeen years he served as director. The Bureau of Prisons was already a national standard setter, but Carlson took a good organization and made it better.
- His style of management guided the Bureau of Prisons effectively throughout one of the most challenging eras in American penal history. The numbers of inmates in prison were skyrocketing. Other challenges included the explosion of inmate gangs, racial conflicts, and drug-trafficking, all of which resulted in more violence in prisons.
- His emphasis on integrity, implemented in both institutions and community-based settings of the Bureau of Prisons, did much to transform the traditional prison culture that had justified the abuse of recalcitrant inmates.
- He supported civil rights and affirmative action before it was politically correct and mandated by law.
- His personal attributes and management style contributed to the outstanding work of the staff, his wardens, and Bureau employees in general.
- He required that inmates be treated with dignity and respect. He believed that inmates respond in kind to how they had been treated.

To put this biography into context, I attended a political rally of a presidential candidate recently and during the question period following his speech, one person said—it is impossible to bring change to this society because we continue with the same problems, regardless of who is in the White House, generation after generation. Yet, what is exciting about Norman A. Carlson's years as Director of the Federal Bureau of Prisons is that he proved it is possible to resolve many of the problems of the past, to meet most of the challenges of the present in innovative ways, and for these changes to continue from one generation to the next. In other words, this biography offers hope that all agencies—and even the government itself—can move forward in providing a better quality of life for its citizens.

Norm Carlson is one of the remarkable leaders in the federal government of the twentieth century. He left his footprint on the world of corrections, and he affected corrections not only on the federal level but also on the state and local levels. Interviewees' comments made it clear that it is about time that his story is told.

Chapter 1

Introduction

The best kept secret in America today is that people would rather work hard for something they believe in than live a life of aimless diversion. . . .

When we raise our sights, strive for excellence, dedicate ourselves to the highest goals of our society, we are enrolling in an ancient and meaningful cause—the age-long struggle of humans to realize the best that is in them.

John W. Gardner[1]

At times we read something or hear something and it has enormous effect on our lives. This happened to Norman A. Carlson, an up-and-coming corrections employee for the Federal Bureau of Prisons, while he was attending a mid-career program at the Woodrow Wilson School of Public and International Affairs, at Princeton University in 1965-1966. In an academic year, in which he heard many lectures and read many books, John W. Gardner's works—*Excellence: Can We Be Equal and Excellent Too?* and *Self-Renewal: The Individual and the Innovative Society*—towered above the rest.[2] The thirty-one-year old Carlson was so struck by Gardner's books that, according to Bureau management officials, they became his "bible of management."[3] At the time, Gardner was the Secretary of Health, Education, and Welfare (now the Department of Health and Human Services), and after leaving government service, he became head of the National Urban Coalition and then founded Common Cause, a nonpartisan citizen's lobby.

Gardner's first book is "concerned with the important business of toning up a whole society, of bringing people to that fine edge of morale and conviction and zest that makes for greatness."[4] Gardner's book on excellence contains a number of inspiring ideas:

- All excellence involves discipline and tenacity of purpose.
- In our own society, one need not search far for an idea of great vitality and power that can and should serve the cause of excellence.
- Our strength, creativity, and growth as a society depend upon our capacity to develop the talents and possibilities of our people.
- Each generation draws from its inherited tradition those values that give strength and continuity to its common life and reinterprets them for contemporary application.
- "Expect a lot." That means have and uphold standards, which are an explicit regard for excellence.
- High individual performance will depend to some extent on the capacity of the society or institution to evolve it.[5]

John Gardner's second book, *Self-Renewal: The Individual and the Innovative Society*, proved to be equally influential on Carlson. It questioned: "How can we design a system that will continually reform itself?"[6] Gardner defines renewal as the "process of bringing results of change into line with our purposes."[7] Later, Gardner talks about innovation as a new way of thinking about things.[8] Gardner contended that "one of the aims of any organization is the development of the individuals who make it up."[9]

Gardner noted that "innovation must be pursued systematically,"[10] Organizing for renewal, according to Gardner, involves developing a system "by which able people are nurtured and moved into positions where they can make their contribution."[11] Another of Gardner's themes became the bulwark of Carlson's prison management style: "If one had to select a single conception that is central to the consensus in our own society, it would be the idea of the dignity and worth of the individual."[12] A further influential dictum on Carlson was Gardner's idea that "Societies are renewed—if they are renewed at all—by people who believe in something, care about something, stand for something."[13]

Norman A. Carlson had five more years to mull over Gardner's ideas before he became Director of the Federal Bureau of Prisons in 1970. When he did become director, he did not have a plan of action as many successful administrators do when they assume the responsibility of running an agency. Yet, what Norm (as he wants everyone to call him) did have is the blueprint that Gardner had laid out in his books. This was directional or suggestive rather than specific.

A Legendary Leader

Norman Carlson's leadership received endorsements from the Bureau of Prisons' staff and those outside the Bureau. Former training director Sam Samples, Ph.D., suggested an appropriate title for this biography, "*A Giant of a Man* or *A Giant of a Leader*. I believe that Norm Carlson could have been President and would have done an excellent job."[14]

Former Warden Rick Seiter, Ph.D., said:

> When you consider all the things that stand out, I don't know if there ever has been a corrections official with such an aura around him, as a corrections leader and visionary as Norm Carlson. There have been few, if any, who had the overall stature and respect that Norm has had. He truly is a legend in his own time. I don't know how far you have to go back to find someone who had such an impact on corrections across the country and internationally.[15]

Former Assistant Director Wade Houk noted: "He was the best there is, and it was an honor to work for him. Since his retirement, he continues to be a presence in corrections, at American Correctional Association meetings, and on the board of directors of The GEO Group, Inc."[16] Former Bureau of Prisons' employee Blake Davis added: "In the world of corrections, Norm Carlson is definitely somebody who has made a dramatic footprint in shaping today's correctional culture. Even years after he has retired, people speak about the tremendous impact he had on our agency."[17]

Michelle Humphrey, Norm's personal secretary the final two years he was Director, remarked on what an impact he had:

> Having worked with three retired directors, Mr. Carlson continues to be the most sought-after director for his opinion, comments, and advice. He is much respected. He always told me that when someone decides to retire, to go out when you are at the top, and he did. Twenty years later people are still calling me to contact him."[18]

William Patrick, whose career in the Bureau focused on the architectural design of new facilities, reported:

> Norm had a vision of what corrections was, a vision of what the Bureau of Prisons ought to be, and a vision of how inmates and staff should be treated. And he never varied from that. It was always crystal clear. He might not have been totally right in everything he did, but he had a vision and worked toward that.[19]

Sherman Day, Ph.D., former director of the National Institute of Corrections and former asisant director of U.S. Bureau of Prisons and later president of Georgia State University, who Norm Carlson persuaded to come and establish a program for staff development and training for the Bureau, provided a more extensive statement in Exhibit 1.1.

Exhibit 1.1 Norm Remains a Pivotal Figure in My Life

"I remember speaking at the fiftieth anniversary of the Bureau in 1980, and [saw] the enormous respect the retirees had for Norm. It was a great occasion in Springfield [Missouri]. The hall was completely filled with people who no longer worked for him. The retirees and people went away thinking that this was a person who could have been President. He fostered great respect not only for him, but [for] the Bureau of Prisons. He created the climate. I am sure former directors of the Bureau did also, but during Norm's years, he really created a source of pride in working for the Bureau of Prisons. They had active retirees' organizations in every institution. You don't find that in most businesses.

"Norm changed a lot of things in the Bureau of Prisons, but he also included former Directors Alexander and Bennett. He kept those people involved. He recognized he lived on their shoulders, and he never disrespected them. Norm made tremendous changes, but he did it without alluding to anything wrong on their part.

"I have never met anyone who didn't have great respect for Norm Carlson. Norm is still one of the giants in my life. I really consider it a special privilege to spend the time I did with Norm in the Bureau of Prisons. It is a great agency. Norm was the right person at the right time. He gave a steadiness to the agency that could have buckled right and left during those times in the early 1970s. Those were tough times."

Source: Interviewed September 2005.

Others outside the Bureau of Prisons also have high praise for Norman Carlson. David Ward, Ph.D., former professor of sociology at the University of Minnesota, commented, "He is one of the finest human beings and public servants I've ever met."[20] Gerald Shur, retired prosecutor in the Criminal Division in the Department of Justice who started the Witness Protection Program in the Department of Justice, said:

> Norm does not realize that he is extraordinary. He assumes that everybody else is competent and capable, just like he is. He makes that assumption. I recall one of the people working with me was introduced to the head of an agency for the first time. This head of the agency said to him,

> 'I supervise x thousand people. How many do you supervise?' Norm would never do that. It would never occur to him.[21]

Two Attorneys General tell what they thought of Norman Carlson's leadership. Former Attorney General Benjamin Civiletti stated:

> I thought that Norman Carlson's contributions to a safe, reasonably and fairly run federal system were extraordinary. My knowledge goes back to the 1960s, when Bobby Kennedy was Attorney General and into the 1980s when I paid attention under Reagan's administration to the Department of Justice activities. In any event, I thought he was the leading head of the Bureau of Prisons, at least through my adult life when I was both a prosecutor and a practicing player.[22]

Former Attorney General Edwin Meese felt that Norm was so effective because he exhibited "the type of leadership that people respected. He had strong personal qualities [that] included a sense of morality. He was in command of the situation at all times."

Meese continued:

> At the same time I think he had compassion and sincere interest in other people, including everyone from the people in the department he was dealing with, but also the administrative staff, line staff, and the inmates. He had a real sense of discipline, and a strong commitment to the mission of the Federal Prison System. I think it was a combination of these qualities that are necessary for the job.[23]

The late Dr. Ruth Westrick Connolly, staff psychiatrist at the Federal Medical Clinic at Rochester, Minnesota, who worked closely with Norm for several years, noted that "Norman Carlson wanted to make a difference. He wanted to show the public that with a humane touch we can actually make a significant difference." She contended:

> [Norm's] message was that we will have fewer riots, less trouble, less breaking out and less demolition within the prison if we feed them well, if we treat them with dignity, and if we keep them busy. We need to treat them like you and I want to be treated. He would admit inmates have transgressed their rights, but there are not many of us who have not done the same. Yes, they are unfortunate to be in prison, but many of them would like to have another chance in life.[24]

For seventeen years, as director of the Federal Bureau of Prisons, Norman Carlson was perceived as one of the best leaders in governmental service. Guided by John Gardner's ideas, he became a legend in his own time. As part of his accomplishments, he kept what was good about the Bureau. He met squarely all the challenges of national corrections. He transformed a federal bureaucracy into a family-like culture; and he and a number of other correctional leaders in state departments of corrections, such as Frank Wood in Minnesota, established an environment where inmates were treated with dignity and respect.

Paradigm Shift

A paradigm shift defines what questions should be asked, how they should be asked, what should be studied, and what rules should be followed in interpreting the obtained answers. As the broadest unit of consensus within a science, a paradigm serves to differentiate one scientific community (or sub-community) from another. A paradigm defines and weaves together the theories, methods, instruments, and exemplars that exist within it.[25]

We might define this as the big "P." However, smaller "p"s, or paradigm shifts, take place when individuals, organizations, and cultures begin to see the world in a new way. These paradigm shifts affect their worldview. These paradigm shifts can involve forming new assumptions and perspectives, raising new questions, and altering behaviors. Thus, paradigm shifts can take place on the individual level, the organizational level, the cultural level within an organization, in the social order, and in the scientific paradigms that govern how the universe operates.

Dr. Ruth Westrick Connolly, who was instrumental in establishing the Federal Medical Center in Rochester as a federal prison, observed:

> I think it was a paradigm shift when Norman Carlson said that locking inmates up and throwing away the key is not really our mission. Our mission is to do our job in the most humane manner, to try to learn from previous mistakes, to attempt to improve what we are doing, and to see what has worked and what has not worked.[26]

When we examine Norman A. Carlson's impact through paradigm shifts, an observer will see that his achievements are remarkable because he made an impact on so many areas:

- The Bureau of Prisons as an organization
- The staff members who worked in the Bureau
- The inmates who were incarcerated
- The response of other governmental agencies to the Bureau, including the Attorney General's Office
- The perception of Congress toward the Bureau
- How the federal judiciary felt about the Director and the Bureau
- The messages, policies, and practices of state correctional systems.

The culture he created within the Bureau of Prisons led staff members to perceive of themselves as family and to be concerned about upholding the basic mission statement of the Bureau, which included maintaining a humane and safe environment for inmates and employees. This culture even had some effect on inmates. Several former staff members claimed that some inmates took more pride in the prison facility, in how it looked, and in what took place within it.

This chapter introduces a biography, which is a study of outstanding leadership. Like his hero Gardner, Norman Carlson wanted to bring out the best in people, wanted to bring out the best in the Bureau of Prisons, and wanted to bring out the best in the Bureau's relationships with other agencies. Unlike Gardner, he did not necessarily extend his visionary leadership to public servants in other areas of government and to the wider society. At a time in which society desperately needs to know that sometimes government works, Norman A. Carlson's service as director of the nation's largest prison system provides that example.

Writing this biography has been a lot of fun. Nearly all of the eighty interviews, which this author conducted, covered the period Norman Carlson served as the Director of the Federal Bureau of Prisons. Almost all the interviews, without exception, provided insightful statements from those who saw the director function at various levels. In addition, I had all the information and more that a biographer would want to examine during the seventeen years he was Director of the Federal Bureau of Prisons. I was able to review fourteen scrapbooks with newspaper clippings, letters, and materials from the archives of the Federal Bureau of Prisons in Washington, D.C.

Endnotes

1. John W. Gardner. 1984 originally published in 1961. *Excellence: Can We Be Equal and Excellent Too? Revised Edition.* New York: W. W. Norton and Co. pp. 155-160.

2. John W. Gardner. 1984 originally published in 1963. *Self-Renewal: The Individual and the Innovative Society.* Revised Edition. New York: W. W. Norton and Co. Gardner, *Equal and Excellent Too.*

3. Interviewed October and November 2005.

4. Gardner, *Equal and Excellent Too*, p. 11.

5. Ibid., pp. 76, 123, 125, 146, 149.

6. Gardner, *Self-Renewal*, p. 5.

7. Ibid., p. 6.

8. Ibid., p. 30.

9. Ibid., p. 65.

10. Ibid., p. 75.

11. Ibid., p. 76.

12. Ibid., p. 86.

13. Ibid., p. 115.

14. Sam Samples, Ph.D., was interviewed October 2005.

15. Rick Seiter, Ph.D., was interviewed August 2005.

16. Wade Houk was interviewed October 2005.

17. Blake Davis was interviewed October 2005.

18. Michelle Humphrey was interviewed December 2005.

19. William Patrick was interviewed September 2005.

20. David Ward, Ph.D., was interviewed March 2006.

21. Gerald Shur was interviewed October 2005.

22. Former Attorney General Benjamin Civiletti was interviewed December 2005.

23. Former Attorney General Edwin Meese was interviewed October 2005.

24. Dr. Ruth Westrick Connolly was interviewed September 2005.

25. Kuhn, Thomas. 1970. *The Structure of Scientific Revolutions, 2nd Edition.* Chicago: The University of Chicago Press.

26. George Ritzer and Douglas Goodman. 2003. *Sociological Theory, 6th ed.* New York: McGraw-Hill.

27. Dr. Ruth Westrick Connolly was interviewed September 2005.

Part I — Personal History

Chapter 2

Life Before the Bureau of Prisons

Norm Carlson is one of our most famous Sioux City ex-residents, and he is very deserving of all the accolades he has received. We were friends as boys, went to the same church, and ran around a lot together. I remember the day that he was appointed director. We were all so proud. Then, when Life *magazine had a story on young Americans on their way up, and Norm was featured in that, we were even prouder.*

Darrell Sea[1]

This chapter examines Norman Carlson's early life until the time he received a position working for the Federal Bureau of Prisons. This includes his years at home, his college years, his experiences in graduate school, and the months he spent as a correctional officer at the Iowa State Penitentiary, in Ft. Madison, Iowa. Not as much material is available on the early stages of his life as there are on the years he was the Director of the Bureau of Prisons.

Early Life

More than one staff member who had worked with Norm for years said, "If you want to know something about Norm Carlson, he is the last person you want to ask." Interestingly, several also noted that they had worked with Norm for years, and he did not talk about personal stuff. Everyone agreed that he had never said anything about his early years.

Norm is a very private person. He never needed to share information or anecdotes about his childhood with anyone, other than his immediate family. He is ready to talk about his first wife, Pat, his present wife, Phyllis, and his two children, Gary and Cindy and their spouses, and his grandchildren. He is proud of his children and what they are doing with their lives. Both of them work in public administration. He is always quick to travel far to attend a football game in which one of his grandsons is playing, or a hockey game in which another grandson is participating.

To respect Norm's desire for privacy, this biography will introduce only a scant outline of his early life. Norm's father, Albert, was a widower with one daughter, Lavonne. He remarried, to Esther, and Norman was born in 1933. His father owned an insurance agency, while Norman's mother stayed at home.

As reflective of the strong Lutheran influence in the home, they attended the Augustana Lutheran Church every Sunday, where his father taught Sunday school. They had the same pew, near the front of the church. In fact, Norm never missed attending Sunday school and/or church, and every year would receive a 100 percent attendance pin.

To demonstrate that young Norman was capable of doing rather ordinary boyhood capers, a friend from childhood, Darrell Sea, who later became the Assistant Superintendent of Schools in Sioux City, recalled: "We had our nickels and pennies for our Sunday School offering, and there were a couple of candy stores, close to the church, and it seems that we would go to the candy store on occasion to spend some of our Sunday school money."[2]

Norm attended Bryant Elementary School, and he then went to North Junior High School in Sioux City. He graduated from Central High, often called the "Castle on the Hill." Central High was a large school, with about 2,000 students when Norm attended.

Norm was always a big kid. He was interested in sports but did not participate in high school athletics. As a high school student, he lived near Hubbard Ball Park and for several years, he was in charge of keeping the ball field in playing shape. He worked very hard, and this is apparently, where he started to develop his softball game. He later became an excellent softball pitcher and volleyball player, and these athletic skills surfaced during his career in the Bureau of Prisons.

Darrell Sea also recalled, "he was a home type, not running the streets, and not wild. He always wanted to do the right thing."[3] According to his friend, the only time he can remember that Norm was ever involved in anything close to wrongdoing was when they were about ten and were on Hill Avenue. During this era, dogcatchers would drive their trucks around and pick up stray dogs. The boys saw a couple of dogs penned up in his truck; the dogcatcher wanted to know who owned one of them. "We made it up, and said that the owner lived around the corner. The dogcatcher had to go around the corner to ask about the dog, and he could not see us." Sea reported, "One of us pulled the pin," but he was not so sure who this was. "Anyhow, we let the dogs out, and then we ran. I would say that is the most trouble he ever got into."[4]

Norm did not have a rebellious streak and did not become involved in delinquent behavior. However, he did form a relationship with Bill Hanson, a police officer who went on to become the Chief of Police in Sioux City. Bill and Norm were very good friends, although Bill was twenty to thirty years older. Norm would occasionally ride along with him. This gave him exposure to law enforcement.

Norm was a good student and was well liked, even though classmates did not appear to know him very well. What contributed to this was that he worked on weekends at a garage that would tow cars. This limited his opportunities for social interaction. As a result, he had few social activities. Sea commented, "I can't remember that he ever had a girlfriend."[5]

Norm's father had no question about what Norm was going to do following his graduation from high school. His father had attended and graduated from Gustavus Adolphus, a small Lutheran College of 2,000 students, in St. Peter, Minnesota. He considered it a quality school, so he decided that his son would go there as well.

Norm emerged from his childhood grounded in terms of having solid family values, a strong faith, and the belief that it was important to do what was right. His sound grounding in basic values served him throughout his career, allowing him to remain steadfast even in challenging times.

College Years

College was a time of awakening for Norm. He started out as a business major, but did not particularly like a course he had in accounting. As a college freshman and putative business major, Norm made C's, but beginning his sophomore year, he became a good student. That year he took an Introduction to Sociology course from Floyd Martinson, Ph.D., which transformed his outlook on higher education. The course so stimulated him that he became a sociology major. He also took Introduction to Criminal Justice from Martinson, which developed his interest in criminology and the criminal justice system.

Later, when Norm Carlson was working for the Federal Bureau of Prisons, Professor Martinson invited Norm to return to Gustavus Adolphus and take a one-year teaching position. Norm considered it, but declined the offer.

He dated Pat Musser during his senior year in college. She was an education major from a farming community in Fairmont, Minnesota. Their relationship become serious as the year went on, and they became engaged following his graduation. They married in September 1956.

Graduate School

The road to corrections for Norm Carlson was not difficult. When he graduated from college, he returned home to Sioux City, Iowa, to pursue an M.A. in sociology from the University of Iowa. During that master's program, he took a course that concentrated on criminology from Professor Robert G. Caldwell, which had a major influence on his career. Professor Caldwell was both a sociologist and an attorney, with appointments in both the Department of Sociology and the School of Law at the University of Iowa. Exhibit 2.1 explains the relationship between Professor Caldwell and his student.

Exhibit 2.1 Professor Robert G. Caldwell and Mentoring of His Students

"Prof. Robert G. Caldwell of the University of Iowa Department of Sociology and Anthropology is exuding a rosy glow of pardonable pride these days.

"It stems from the recent elevation of one of his former students, Norman A. Carlson, to the position of director of the Federal Bureau of Prisons, succeeding Myrl E. Alexander. (Alexander retired this year after 35 years in the Bureau).

"Carlson, 36, a native of Sioux City, earned his MA degree in criminology under Prof. Caldwell at UI in 1957. For the past four years he has served as executive assistant to Alexander.

"As Carlson's former mentor and adviser, Caldwell could well be pleased with comments made by U.S. Attorney General John N. Mitchell in announcing the new appointment:

> 'Norm Carlson by background, training, and dedication is the most qualified man to take over this critical position. I am confident that he will move the prison system forward helping to break the cycle of recidivism that has plagued our criminal justice system. If we can curtail recidivism, we can have a great impact upon crime in this country.'

> 'Under Norm Carlson's leadership, we intend to make the federal prison system into an even better model which can help our states improve their correctional systems more rapidly, a goal which we have given the highest priority.'

"Caldwell acted quickly to congratulate the new appointee."
The acknowledgement he received from Carlson reads in part:
'As a former student of yours, I want to personally express my appreciation for what you did to get me started in this career. I'm sure you realize that had it not been for your suggestion that I spend a summer at Fort Madison all that which has happened would have been impossible. Thanks again for your sound counsel and advice!'

"The reference to Fort Madison points to a significant aspect of the criminology program that Caldwell has developed during his more than twenty years at the University of Iowa. Working closely with the state's penal and correctional institutions, he has encouraged graduate students to seek summer jobs as guards or in other capacities at Fort Madison, to learn firsthand how a modern prison is run. Others have combined similar employment with field work at Anamosa and Eldora."

Source: Johanna Beers. 1978. "UI Criminologist Pleased over Ex-Student's Success: Cooperative Programs with Penal Institutions: Recalled," *Press-Citizen*, Wednesday, April 29. Used with permission.

Norm spent the summer of 1956 working as a correctional officer at the Iowa State Penitentiary at Fort Madison. This is a nineteenth-century penitentiary, with high cement walls, small cells, and austere surroundings. Carlson lived rent free in the "Boar's Nest," living quarters for single correctional officers. In his spare time, he worked on his master's thesis, which examined the work patterns of inmates at a small conservation camp (near the Iowa State Penitentiary).

One of the highlights that summer was conversations which Alan Atwood, William Nardini, and Norman Carlson had with the warden, Percy Lainson, a former county sheriff and army colonel. The warden would come out from his home at night to smoke on a bench in the backyard, because his wife would not permit smoking in the house. While he rolled his Bull Durhams, Professor Caldwell's three students were ready to learn from this seasoned corrections veteran.

Percy Lainson freely dispensed his correctional wisdom while he was smoking, but he had an ulterior motive. He was hopeful that at least one of the men would return to work at the institution. "We were in dire need of such men," he commented. "They did a magnificent job for us."[6]

Norm reflects on that first summer at the Iowa State Penitentiary:

That first summer I worked as a uniformed correctional officer, actually as a relief officer. We had two days off during the week, and we always worked weekends. As I recall, I got all of the dirty jobs that nobody else wanted because I was a college kid. I remember on Saturday mornings I always had to sit in a big tall chair outside the inmates' showers. It was steamy and hot, and I had to watch those guys come in. They got their weekly shower, and it was a long shower. Those guys would come parading down there in the nude. They had to drop their clothes off, go to the shower, and get their clean clothes from the other end. It was like an assembly line. It wasn't a pleasant place to spend your Saturdays. I worked down on death row once or twice. It was a good experience because I worked all over the institution and had a taste of everything.[7]

Both Nardini and Carlson did return to work at the Iowa State Penitentiary. Nardini went on to get his Ph.D. at Iowa, and later served as associate warden of classification and treatment at the Iowa State Penitentiary; then, he became Delaware's first Commissioner of Corrections. He went on to become the first chairperson of the newly established Department of Criminology at Indiana State University.

Carlson had another experience in graduate school that contributed to his career. He took a course from Frederick E. Haynes, author of the well-known book, *The American Prison System*.[8] During one of Haynes' lectures, he pointed out that whenever he went to a prison, he would go up to a line officer, or correctional officer, and ask how things were going. If this officer were inarticulate or discourteous, Professor Haynes found that this was reflective of institutional disorder or problems. However, if the officer were courteous and treated him with respect, then Haynes found that this was a barometer that things were going pretty well in the institution.

Norm understood early on how important it was to talk with line staff. Later, when he became director and regularly visited the Bureau's prisons, he always talked with line officers.

Iowa Department Of Corrections

Norm received his degree at the end of the winter quarter in early February, and he was promised a job when he graduated. He went to work at Fort Madison in the winter of 1957. Norm had regular contact with inmates and came to understand the problems of confinement in a maximum-security facility. As he interacted with correctional officers, he saw that some were far less than committed to their jobs and some occasionally engaged in incidents of brutality toward inmates. He also observed Warden Lainson, and his admiration for him increased rather than decreased with greater contact.

Norm Carlson was one of the two treatment staff who was hired at this time. Norm's title was "sociologist." His job was to prepare social history reports on inmates. He interviewed prisoners, recorded significant events that had occurred in their lives, and prepared classification reports. About these, he told the author, "The ironic thing is that nobody ever used these reports, but it was believed that it was a progressive institution and you had to do it."[9] A psychologist was the other treatment person hired. The job of the psychologist was to administer a battery of psychological tests, such as the MMPI and others.

Another experience Carlson had at Ft. Madison was preparing reports on inmates who were going before the parole board, which came to the institution about every three months. The reports focused on inmates' conduct: how they behaved while they were locked up. In addition, he was in charge of the Alcoholics Anonymous chapter. This institution had a large AA group that met on Saturday mornings and once every week at night. Norm noted, "Hundreds of inmates would show up in the audience on Saturday, and we probably had the largest AA chapter of any prison in the nation. We would have speakers come from the outside."[10]

He eventually became aware that the then-chairperson of the Iowa Parole Board was the wife of a reformed alcoholic. As Carlson remembers it, her father was an alcoholic, too. She saw redemption through the use of AA. When the inmates figured this out, they all claimed to be alcoholics who had seen the error of their ways. They were quick to assure everyone, especially the parole board, that they would never drink again.

One day, while interviewing a new inmate, the inmate suggested that Carlson consider working for the Federal Bureau of Prisons. The inmate said that it would be a better job in a more progressive system. Norm thought about it. He was married by this time, and Pat and he were thinking of starting a family. So, in 1958, he took a Federal Service Entrance Exam.

Norm passed the test and received a job offer as a real estate appraiser. This was not quite what he had in mind, so he wrote a letter to the Civil Service System telling them he wanted to work in a federal prison. A few months later, he received a job offer to be a parole officer in the U.S. Penitentiary in Leavenworth, Kansas, which he accepted.

Conclusion

We learn from this chapter that Norman Carlson came from a stable family background. Faith was important to him. The strength he received from his background provided a firm foundation for the career that followed. In addition, he was fortunate to have a professor in graduate school who referred him to the Iowa State Penitentiary, where he met Percy Lainson, a warden. Lainson offered him a job following the completion of his graduate program, and his career in corrections was off and running.

Endnotes

1. Darrrell Sea was interviewed June 2006.

2. Ibid.

3. Ibid.

4. Ibid.

5. Ibid.

6. Beer, Johanna. 1978. "UI Criminologist Pleased over Ex-Student's Success: Cooperative Programs with Penal Institutions Recalled." *Press Citizen*. April 29.

7. Carlson was interviewed in 2006.

8. Frederick E. Haynes. 1939. *The American Prison System*. New York: McGraw-Hill.

9. Norm Carlson was interviewed July 2005.

10. Norm Carlson was interviewed September 2006.

Chapter 3

Fast Rise to the Top: 1957-1969

He was a guy who everybody said was going to do great things. In his twenties he was being portrayed in this way, mainly because he was a standout. You listened to him and talked to him; you could tell that he was an extremely bright guy. He had a very clear mission in corrections—to make the Bureau of Prisons the best corrections system. He wanted to be the best. And he accomplished that goal. He never lost sight of his mission.

He was able to inspire staff in so many ways. I think it goes back to 'My people are important, I am going to remember their face and name.' Before Norm, the directors were stand-offish. You could not get close to those folks. They were traditional types of managers, typical Washington bureaucrats, I mean that in a good way. But Norm wasn't that way! It was an honor to be his friend, and it was a privilege to work for him. I will never have another boss like him.

Steve Grzegorek[1]
Former Bureau of Prisons Regional Director

Norman Carlson began his service as a parole officer in the U.S. Penitentiary in Leavenworth, Kansas in 1957. For the next thirteen years, he made a rapid rise, until he was appointed Director of the Bureau in 1970. These years are reviewed in the first part of the chapter; the second part of the chapter documents the excellence of the Bureau of Prisons even before Norm became director. Directors Sanford Bates, James V. Bennett, and Myrl Alexander, the three directors who preceded Norm, were all outstanding leaders. So, when Carlson became Director of the Bureau of Prisons, it was already acknowledged to be a standard setter in American corrections. He did not have to clean up a corrections agency that was in a horrific mess; instead, he took a fine agency and led it to become a better agency.

U.S. Penitentiary in Leavenworth, Kansas

Norman Carlson remained at Leavenworth, a huge and well-organized facility, for almost two years. Carlson considered its administration very professional. His job as a parole officer was to interview inmates and to submit reports to institutional classification and the U.S. Board of Parole. This report identified what the inmate had done, included his conduct record, the job he had held, and how much schooling he had completed—work that would be done by a caseworker today. Six parole officers had responsibility for the 2,500 inmates incarcerated at Leavenworth.

One of his experiences was on an Emergency Response Squad. Today, this group is known as a SWAT team. He was the only non-correctional officer, but was picked for this assignment because he was big and athletic. The team received training one day a month; the inmates, according to Carlson, called them "the goon squad." The only time they were called into service was when inmates would walk off from the minimum-security camp. However, the emergency squad was also prepared to suit up and take appropriate action if an emergency arose inside the penitentiary.[2]

The Federal Correctional Institution, Ashland, Kentucky

Bureau Director James Bennett was instrumental in having Congress pass the Youth Corrections Act. Ashland, Kentucky, and Englewood, Colorado, were facilities established to house youthful offenders. Both were considered experimental and used indeterminate sentencing. Norm received an offer for promotion to the

Federal Correctional Institution at Ashland, Kentucky, which at the time was a facility for youthful offenders. Pat, his wife, was pregnant, and they were not too excited about going to Kentucky because Pat wanted to return to teaching, and teaching jobs did not appear to be available in Ashland.

Carlson wanted to go to Englewood, Colorado, but did not receive an offer there. Six months later, Ashland called again, and Norm knew that he had to accept the job or it might be the last offer he would receive. In those days, the Bureau of Prisons did not have an application process; all decisions were made in Washington, D.C.

Norm Carlson's job at the Federal Correctional Institution at Ashland was as a casework supervisor. His main task was to supervise six other caseworkers and, as a mid-level manager, the caseworkers reported to him. He also sponsored the institution's Jaycees chapter for inmates, becoming a member of the downtown Jaycees. At Ashland, Norm began to hone his softball pitching skills.

Department of Justice, Washington, D.C.

Norm was detailed to Washington, D.C. for two months in 1960 and became a staff assistant in the classification bureau. Director Bennett had come across Carlson, liked him, and wanted him to come to Washington to gain experience at the central office level. In this assignment, Norm assisted in handling the Alcatraz caseload, in terms of who would be placed on the "Rock" and who would be transferred to other prisons, and drafted letters for Director Bennett. When a frustrated judge or a member of Congress wrote to the director, Norm would get the necessary information and respond to the letter for the director.

In 1961, he was appointed to be the director of the four halfway houses that the Bureau developed that year. These halfway houses were called "Community Treatment Centers," and were the brainchild of Attorney General Robert Kennedy. This brought the Carlsons to Washington on a permanent assignment.

Director Bennett was seventy-years old; yet, he wanted to stay on. J. Edgar Hoover, director of the FBI at the time and a rival of

Bennett's for decades, also wanted to stay on and avoid retirement. As it turned out, Hoover stayed on and died in office, but Bennett had to retire at the mandatory age of seventy. Norm learned another valuable lesson—get out on top. Do not stay beyond your capacity to serve well.

The third Director of the Bureau of Prisons, Myrl Alexander, had worked in the Bureau for many years and had returned to teaching at Southern Illinois University. When he came to Washington, D.C. to assume his new position in 1964, he decided to keep Norm Carlson in his office as Executive Assistant to the Director. Norm assumed new responsibilities, one of which was to respond to inquiries from members of Congress. He got to know members of Congress, including members of the Senate Judiciary Committee. Having demonstrated that he could handle this type of sensitive assignment, Alexander was impressed and so were others.

Former Warden George C. Wilkinson reported, "From what I knew of him, he was pretty much a hard charger and an outstanding individual before he became director. He was the executive assistant to the director when he returned to Washington, D.C."[3]

Bureau staff were not surprised when Myrl Alexander decided to retire. He had been involved with the Bureau for thirty-seven years, and was ready to return to Southern Illinois University and resume teaching there. Considerable discussion occurred about whom Alexander's successor would be, and at least one Bureau official was convinced that he would be the choice. The wardens of the federal prisons had their own ideas, but none thought that Norman Carlson, only thirty-six years old, who had never served as an associate warden or a warden, had a chance of being selected.

Yet, Norman Carlson had met the approval of a committee appointed to choose the new director and Attorney General John Mitchell had approved the committee's recommendation. Carlson had been selected to become a federal warden and was ready to assume the new job when he was appointed director.

The Legacy of Strong Leadership

(Left to right) Sanford Bates, James V. Bennett, Myrl E. Alexander, and Norman A. Carlson, on the occasion of Carlson's swearing in as Director of the Bureau of Prisons. (Bureau of Prisons)

One of Norman A. Carlson's attributes as a leader is that he built on the strengths that were already present in the Bureau of Prisons. He recognized the leadership capacities of Sanford Bates, James Bennett, and Myrl Alexander, former directors of the Bureau of Prisons who were still alive when Carlson became director in 1970. However, much more significantly, Carlson recognized the strong foundation in the Bureau that he had inherited, freely gave credit to this substantial history of the Bureau, and proceeded to build on it. He genuinely believed that it was his honor to be part of this proud history and to be one of those who would carry this quality agency from the past to the present.

The way that Carlson tied the past into the present, building on the strengths of the past, became one of the features of his leadership. He had an amazing ability to build on continuity, while amending it with the necessities of the present landscape, and, at the same time, to plan for and project the future.

A Brief History of the Federal Bureau of Prisons

The history of the Federal Bureau of Prisons can be divided into the periods from about 1890 to 1930 when the Bureau came into existence; to the time that Sanford Bates was appointed director until he retired; to the time that James Bennett succeeded him until he retired; and to the time that Myrl E. Alexander was appointed director to his retirement in 1970. Norman A. Carlson replaced him and became the fourth director of the Bureau. This began a new era for the Federal Bureau of Prisons.

Early History of Federal Prisons. There were federal prisoners soon after the birth of the federal government in 1789. The federal government encouraged states to enact legislation to confine individuals convicted of federal crimes in state prisons.[4] With the creation of the Department of Justice in 1870, federal inmates came under the authority of the Attorney General.[5] A general agent managed the federal prisoners for the Attorney General, a position that eventually evolved into that of the Superintendent of Prisons. The Superintendent of Prisons answered to an Assistant Attorney General and was responsible for the custody and care of all federal prisoners.[6] During this period, the federal government maintained no prisons or federal jails, but boarded federal prisoners in local or state facilities.[7]

The contemporary history of the Federal Prison System began in 1891, following Congress' passage of the Three Prisons Act. By the beginning of the twentieth century, the federal government started to provide its own prison cells. Construction was underway at Atlanta, Georgia, and Leavenworth, Kansas, and the old territorial prison at McNeil Island in Washington had received regular penitentiary status. The Atlanta Penitentiary opened in January 1902 on a 300-acre site, with total accommodation for 1,200 prisoners. Work began in 1897 on the Leavenworth Penitentiary, but it was not completed until 1906, at which time the old military prison at Fort Leavenworth was returned to the War Department. Leavenworth had a planned capacity of 1,200 prisoners. The three institutions represented the penal investment of the federal government until 1925. In the 1920s, the government built a reformatory at Chillicothe, Ohio, and a prison for women at Alderson, West Virginia. However, there was still no bureaucracy, and no effective supervisory force to form a prison system.[8]

The responsibility of the federal facilities fell upon the shoulders of Attorney General Harlan F. Stone, with his progressively minded assistant, Mabel Walker Willebrandt. At the time, a handful of individuals in the Department of Justice had the task of supervising federal institutions, recommending the parole of inmates to the Attorney General, and inspecting jails. In 1929, aware that the care of prisoners needed more consideration, a committee of the House of Representatives made a thorough study. They reported that the time had arrived for the establishment of a Bureau of Prisons, the construction of several new institutions, and the passage of legislation that would result in the organization of an integrated federal penal system.[9]

With the active support of President Herbert Hoover and Attorney General William DeWitt Mitchell, staffers prepared legislation presented before Congress in December 1929. Upon hearing of the crowded conditions and of the need for the development of both parole and probation systems in the federal government, Congress adopted every recommendation of the Department of Justice, giving birth to the Federal Bureau of Prisons.[10]

This legislation defined the duties and powers of the Bureau. It projected the development of a complete prison system with classified institutions. It also authorized a new penitentiary and an additional reformatory. It also established a Board of Parole and expanded the Federal Probation Law. Enabling regulations considered a hospital for the care of the insane and the sick. The regulations instructed the U.S. Public Health Service to provide medical and psychiatric services to federal penal facilities. The legislation called for planning for the construction of a few federal jails. Additionally, Congress passed an act calling for the installation of a diversified system of prison industries.[11]

Sanford Bates, First Director, 1930-1937. Sanford Bates, the director of the Massachusetts prison system, became Federal Superintendent of Prisons in 1929. Not surprisingly, Bates, known as a reformer and a well-respected administrator, became the first Director of the Bureau of Prisons in 1930. Bates and his young aides wanted to make certain that the enabling legislation made the director's position a strong one. They had already witnessed the failure of California's newly formed Department of Penology headed by a director whose formal power was limited to calling a meeting of five deputies once a month.[12]

Legislation granted the director of the Bureau of Prisons the power to hire and fire wardens and other personnel. Prison staff for the first time came under Civil Service regulations. Staff found guilty of brutality were demoted or terminated. Staff who bucked the agency's official commitment to the "individualized care and custody" of prisoners did so only once before they had to find new jobs during the dreary days of the Great Depression. Bates also strengthened the agency by rallying political support for it by using his personal connections to Republican Party figures, including former President Calvin Coolidge.[13]

With his impressive administrative background, Sanford Bates intended to begin a legacy of strong leadership in the Bureau of Prisons. *Prisons and Beyond*, a book he wrote in 1936, describes his beliefs on institutional leadership. Bates believed that in contrast to the nation's dismal prisons, with often brutal staff, the Bureau of Prisons' custodial institutions would provide a degree of humane confinement unusual for the time. Bates continually stated that the Bureau of Prisons—while still maintaining custodial institutions—would provide humane confinement.

James V. Bennett, Second Director, 1937-1964. In 1937, James V. Bennett succeeded Bates and directed the agency for the next twenty-seven years. Bennett was a management specialist in the Bureau of Efficiency (the forerunner of the Office of Management and

Budget). He was on the team that investigated conditions inside federal prisons for the Cooper Commission and, in fact, wrote most of the Commission's report.[14]

Bennett laid the groundwork politically on which Federal Prison Industries (known since 1978 as UNICOR) was built. Despite fierce opposition to the production and sale of prison-made goods, Bennett persuaded and compromised his way to centralizing the formerly scattered federal prison industries. Today, UNICOR employs tens of thousands of federal prisoners. It is a multimillion-dollar enterprise producing goods from Army helmets and clothes to highway signs and furniture.[15]

Bennett also guided the development of an inmate classification system. The system intended to rationalize prisoner management and to promote individualized treatment. This classification system was far ahead of anything else used at the time, and elements of it remain in the classification instrument, still used by the Bureau of Prisons (and emulated by many states).[16]

Bennett further reduced institutional regimentation. He oversaw the building of clean, open, and modern institutions; developed meaningful work opportunities for inmates; improved educational and vocational training programs; provided diagnostic and counseling services; and instituted halfway house programs.[17]

Bennett became the agency's "public face" and chief spokesperson for nearly the next thirty years. He was able to cultivate positive relationships with the attorney general, key judges, policymakers on the Hill, and academic opinion makers. He also developed a recruiting and training program for agency workers, instituted award programs for institutional personnel, and was sensitive to the needs of line staff. In addition, he became involved in international corrections activities through the United Nations and pioneered new correctional concepts, such as individualized treatment programs, and special programs for community corrections and for youth.[18]

Finally, Bennett became a director who paid great attention to detail; some staff would say he paid too much attention to small detail. He was concerned that interviews of prospective employees might be perfunctory and that too many staff members were overweight. He believed that administrators should limit the amount of gasoline allowed in institution trucks to make it impossible for inmates to steal the gasoline and make highballs. He outlawed staff keeping pets on the reservation (institutional campus). He thought that staff permitted inmates to watch too much television. He said that institutions should cease awarding cigarettes as prizes in inmate athletic competitions. He also was concerned with unnecessary duplications of inmate files.[19]

Myrl Alexander, Third Director, 1964-1970. Myrl Alexander carried on Bennett's strong leadership when he directed the agency for the next six years. Director Alexander had an extremely impressive background. He served as a staff member in several Bureau of Prisons' institutions, including in associate warden and warden positions. He was the Chief of Prisons, in the Military Government for Germany, 1945-1946; and he had been Assistant Director in the Bureau of Prisons, 1947-1961. This meant that he had spent plenty of time in Bennett's enormous shadow. He had served as president of the American Correctional Association in 1956. He was the founder and a professor of the Center for the Study of Crime, Delinquency, and Corrections, Southern Illinois University, and a professor at the University of Florida.

Alexander successfully consolidated many of the gains that Bennett had made, and initiated a few innovations of his own. In fact, Alexander's legacy was that of a correctional change and reform agent. In a speech he gave as part of his presidential address to the American Correctional Association he expressed his spirit of reform in "A Bill of Rights for the Person under Restraint in a Free Democratic Society":

1. The *right* to clean, decent surroundings with competent attention to his physical and mental well-being.
2. The *right* to maintain and reinforce the strengthening ties which bind him to his family and to his community.

3. The *right* to develop and maintain skills as a productive worker in our economic system.
4. The *right* to fair, impartial, and intelligent treatment without special privilege or license for any man.
5. The *right* to positive guidance and counsel from correctional personnel possessed of understanding and skill.

In sum, Director Alexander was the third strong director of the Bureau of Prisons. All had very positive periods of administration. All three had clarity about their correctional mission, had support from the President and the Attorney General's office, believed in individualized treatment of inmates, discouraged inmate abuse, and supported staff training. Under their leadership, the Bureau of Prisons set a high benchmark for state and local systems of corrections. Most correctional personnel considered the Bureau of Prisons the best corrections system in the United States, a model for others.

What Made the Bureau of Prisons into a Good Agency?

Paul W. Keve, former Director of Delaware Department of Corrections and a professor at the Virginia Commonwealth University, authored an excellent history of the Bureau of Prisons, *Prisons and the American Conscience: A History of U.S. Federal Corrections*. He described the innovations that established the Bureau of Prisons as a good or standard-setting agency:

- Employing merit not patronage in the hiring of directors and staff
- Viewing inmates as individuals
- Building a system to be emulated
- Creating a corporation for prison industries
- Supporting Community Corrections
- Establishing Unit Management

Employing Merit not Patronage in the Hiring of Directors and Staff. In the late 1920s, when Assistant Attorney General Mabel Walker Willebrandt looked for a progressive administrator to head the anticipated Bureau of Prisons, she was ready to forego the long accommodation to the political patronage system. She was ready to hire the best person she could find and was willing to consider professional expertise ahead of party affiliation. This repudiation of patronage practices turned out to be a conspicuous innovation for the federal prison system. The Bureau of Prisons kept patronage out of the appointments of the first three directors, and at no time in the seventy-seven year history of the agency has there been a serious attempt to restore the patronage practice.[21]

Viewing Inmates as Individuals, as People. While the professionalism of the prison system was the first and most significant thrust of Bates, he also contributed an individualized treatment philosophy for the management of prisoners. Both Bennett and Alexander continued this treatment approach, incorporating prisoner classification processes, decent food and housing, and vocational and educational programs, and counseling interventions. Seeing the value of inmates as individuals characterized the leadership of all three directors.[22]

Building a System to be Emulated. From the very beginning of Bates' leadership, through the next two directors and extending to the present, the Bureau of Prisons has built a correctional system that state and local systems of corrections attempt to emulate. The Bureau accomplished this role, not by interfering in the leadership of other corrections systems, but by providing the standard of progressive prison management and by acting as a clearinghouse for information and prison statistics.[23]

Creating a Corporation for Prison Industries in a World of Free Enterprise. One of Bennett's accomplishments was his creation of a separate corporation to operate prison industries. He persuaded Congress to create an independent corporation to operate the industries of the federal prisons. He allied the usual opponents by having the corporation board governed by five members including prominent leaders from labor, agriculture, management, and the public. The bill, which established the Federal Prison Industries, passed with a minimum of opposition after President Franklin Delano Roosevelt negotiated support from labor leaders.[24]

Supporting Community Corrections. The Bureau of Prisons has supported the community corrections movement since the early 1960s. A precipitating factor was newly appointed Attorney General, Robert F. Kennedy, advising Director Bennett of his willingness to find funds for any innovative new approaches the Bureau might propose. The Bureau came up with several significant programs, including their version of halfway houses called "Prerelease Guidance Centers." Centers soon opened in Chicago, Los Angeles, and New York. Soon after that, three others opened in Detroit, Kansas City, and Washington, D.C. All of the pre-release guidance centers operated under the supervision of future Bureau director Norman A. Carlson.

Establishing Unit Management. A clash between custody and treatment has long plagued prison management. In this dichotomy, the two types of staff divide every prison as they work against each other. During the early 1960s, the federal system began developing a management approach to deal with this problem. Staff members from both groups were delegated a combination of both treatment and control functions in defined inmate living areas. The staff team then became responsible for governing all aspects of inmates' lives. This system was initially used at the National Training School for Boys in Washington, D.C. (closed when Morgantown, West Virginia was opened); Ashland, Kentucky; Englewood, Colorado; and El Reno, Oklahoma.[25] During the time that Norman Carlson was the fourth director of the Bureau, 1970-1987, he oversaw the expansion of unit management to all of the federal facilities. For further discussion of unit management, see Chapter 9.

Conclusions

The Bureau of Prisons was fortunate to appoint three competent administrators as directors. Each of them wanted to develop a system of corrections that treated inmates decently, emphasized the training of staff, provided educational and vocational programs for inmates, constructed new and modern prisons, developed extensive prison industries, and established community-based pre-release centers.

During his career, Carlson was twice selected to return to an institution, once as associate warden and once as warden. For various reasons, neither transfer worked. By the time that Norman A. Carlson received his appointment as director in 1970, the Bureau of Prisons had become a good agency. There was a continuity of outstanding leadership at the top, support from the Attorney General's office and Congress, and sound public relations in the community. The first three directors had remained on the job long enough to establish a strong tradition of competent leadership.

Still, it is a long way from serving a summer internship at the Iowa State Penitentiary, living in a fairly primitive officers' dormitory, to becoming the Director of the Bureau of Prisons. Norm Carlson's move up the ladder these thirteen years was rapid. He went from being a correctional officer at the Iowa State Penitentiary, to a parole officer at the U.S. Penitentiary, Leavenworth, to a caseworker and caseworker supervisor at Ashland Youth Center, to various responsibilities in Washington, D.C. In the ten years he spent in Washington, D.C., he supervised the four community treatment centers or halfway houses run by the Bureau of Prisons.

However, it was the time that he spent assisting Director Bennett and later Director Alexander that proved to be so instrumental to his rapid career climb. In whatever they asked him to do, Norm simply did it, and did it very well.

In 1965, halfway through the decade he spent in Washington, D.C., he was selected to be a mid-career fellow at the Woodrow Wilson School of Public and International Affairs in Princeton. He had been selected to return to an institution as an associate warden when he was chosen to attend the mid-career fellowship. That year prepared him in many ways for the challenging job of directing a major federal agency.

During that year, he became convinced that excellence would be the theme of his career in the Bureau of Prisons. He learned that the

Bureau of Prisons had a distinguished history in so many ways and he became convinced that it could become an even better agency. With the appointment of Norman Carlson, the leadership passed to an individual who built on what was good about the Bureau of Prisons but provided the quality of leadership that enabled the Bureau to become an even better agency.

Endnotes

1. Steve Grzegorek was interviewed August 2005.

2. Ibid.

3. George C. Wilkinson was interviewed October 2005.

4. Paul W. Keve. 1991. *Prisons and the American Conscience: A History of U.S. Federal Corrections*. Carbondale and Edwardsville: Southern Illinois University Press. p. xiii.

5. Ibid.

6 Ibid.

7. Ibid., p. xiv.

8. John W. Roberts, ed. 1990. "View from the Top," *Federal Prisons Journal 1*, Summer, p. 28.

9. Ibid.

10. Ibid.

11. Ibid.

12. John J. DiIulio. 1990. "Prisons That Work," *Federal Prisons Journal 1*, Summer, p. 9.

13. Ibid.

14. Ibid., p. 9.

15. Ibid. p. 10.

16. Ibid., p. 9.

17. John W. Roberts. 1994. "Grand Designs, Small Details: The Management Style of James V. Bennett, *Federal Prisons Journal 3*, Winter, p. 29.

18. DiIulio, "Prisons That Work," p. 10.

19. Roberts, "Grand Designs, Small Details," p. 30.

20. Roberts, ed., "View from the Top," p. 37.

21. Paul W. Keve. 1994. "The Sources of Excellence," *Federal Prisons Journal 3*, Winter, p. 11.

22. Ibid., p. 12.

23. Ibid.

24. Ibid., p. 13.

25. Ibid.

Chapter 4

The Buck Stops Here: The Turbulent 1970s

Norm certainly fit the picture of a Director of the Bureau of Prisons. His physical size, his crew cut, his powerful presence were always more than enough to impress and intimidate anyone in his presence, especially a lowly employee. He had no patience for phony or insincere attempts to win his favor, and had a very low tolerance for incompetence. On the other hand, he seemed uncanny in his ability to recognize talent and was quick to acknowledge good work. He was legendary in his ability to remember the names of staff and that meant a great deal to staff at the institutions.

Norm's ability to stay above the fray during controversial times in corrections is the result of many of the characteristics I've already noted. Having served as Director for more than ten years myself, I used Norm as my role model very frequently. Norm taught me to always remember who we work for in the Bureau of Prisons. He knew to stay keenly aware of our relationship with the administration we served, the federal judiciary, the Congress, the inmate advocacy groups, and the inmates themselves. Norm would approach controversial issues very directly, and his straightforward, candid approach would serve to avoid the emotionalism that would often surround issues of corrections. His position was always well informed, based on substance, and supported by actual practice. He was respected by those he worked for as much as by those who worked for him. His loyalty and his ability were unquestioned.

Kathleen Hawk Sawyer, director of the Federal Bureau of Prisons, 1992-2003[1]

Norman A. Carlson was director of the Federal Bureau of Prisons for seventeen years from 1970-1987. These were turbulent years for corrections in the United States, and the Bureau of Prisons had to deal with inmate racial conflicts and violence, the politicization of prisoners, institutional disorder and riots, the growth of the federal inmate population, and the need for additional facilities to house them. With directors and commissioners of corrections in many state agencies going through revolving doors, sometimes every year or two, Norman Carlson held his job through four Presidents and a greater number of Attorneys General.

He intended to retire a year before he did, but Edwin Meese, then Attorney General, wanted him to stay a year longer and groom his successor, which he did. In 1987, at his retirement dinner, nearly everyone in the corrections world, federal, state, and local, hailed him as an outstanding leader of an excellent agency. Equally significantly, the members of Congress who had worked with Norm or heard his presentations on the Hill and the various Attorneys General and their Associate and Assistant Attorneys General affirmed the outstanding nature of his leadership.

This chapter documents the period from his appointment as director in 1970 to 1979; the following chapter records some of the major events that took place from 1980 to his retirement in 1987. Other chapters examine some of the paradigm shifts that Norman Carlson's leadership accomplished.

The First Decade

On Wednesday, March 25, 1970, Attorney General John N. Mitchell appointed Norman A. Carlson as the fourth director of the Federal Bureau on Prisons. There was great surprise, even shock, in response to this announcement. Washington, D.C. is known as a place where few secrets are kept, and appointments of senior government officials are almost always known ahead of time. However, it is safe to say his appointment was a surprise to all the "insiders."

Before leaving the office on his first day as director, Norm wrote a letter to Bureau staff, in which he addressed this matter of his leadership (*see* Exhibit 4.1).

Exhibit 4.1 To Wardens, Superintendents, and Youth Center Directors

"Before leaving the office today, I wanted to write a brief note and share some of my thoughts and reactions to the Attorney General's decision that was announced this morning.

"In a real sense, the appointment is a tribute to the entire career service in the Bureau of Prisons and not to me personally. The confidence which the Attorney General expressed was directed to an organization which has been built on a solid foundation by my three predecessors—Sanford Bates, Jim Bennett, and Alex. Without their vision, dedication and leadership nothing we have done in the past or will accomplish in the future could have been possible. The organization today is a tribute to them and their careers.

"As I am certain you realize, these past several months have been extremely trying in many respects. The uncertainty that existed regarding the Director's position, the 1971 Budget Hearings, the brutal assault on officers at Lewisburg, and the proposed take over of the Lorton Reformatory have all presented problems of major proportion. During this frustrating period of time, Gus Moeller did an outstanding job of keeping the organization moving under difficult circumstances. I know you join me in expressing our appreciation for a job well done! I personally feel relieved to know that Gus will continue to be sitting in the next office sharing responsibility for the job ahead.

"As for the future, there is much to be done in the months ahead. Foremost, is the necessity of finding replacements for Allen Childers at Englewood and Blackie [Olin Blackwell] at Atlanta. In addition, we have to complete work on the ten year plan and other items included in the President's Directive on Corrections. The continuing increase in population is producing problems in nearly every institution. Even greater is the problem of militancy which is beginning to spill over in our institutions.

"During the next few months, I hope to visit as many institutions as possible. We are planning a Wardens' Conference as soon as possible, probably in late April or early May. I'll let you know the details as soon as plans are completed.

"In closing, let me express my personal appreciation for the assistance and support you have displayed in the past. I pledge to do all in my power to continue the work of the Federal Prison System."

Norm A. Carlson,
Director

In this first correspondence from the director's office, which he signed "Norm," he gives some indication of the leader he would be. The letter is humble. He is, he suggests, the appointed leader of a great organization, and his primary objective is to continue the legacy it has. He gives credit to the leadership of Gus Moeller, who was the one most predicted to be the next director of the Bureau. He let everyone know that he was not only cognizant of the challenges the Bureau faced in the present and immediate future, but he intended to provide positive leadership. In announcing the Wardens' Conference to come, he promised that Bureau staff would have a better sense of what he had in mind for the Bureau's new directions.

Norm Carlson revealed strong leadership traits from the time he was sworn in. He had a commanding presence, a blend of genuine humility and willingness to always give others credit for the accomplishments of the Bureau, and he was ready to take charge. Norm's presence was probably helped, of course, by his height of 6' 4", his crew cut, and his no-nonsense demeanor.

It was evident from the beginning that he was a decision-maker. He would look at a situation, listen to staff members' explanations, and be able to make a quick decision that Bureau employees learned was almost always correct. It was not long before wardens and those in Bureau headquarters came to the conclusion that he was ahead of the curve. He saw with remarkable accuracy problems that the Bureau would be facing down the road.

Bureau employees also became aware that Norm was committed to excellence. He intended to make certain that the Bureau would lead corrections. This commitment to excellence included the appearance of a hands-on management style for wardens, and an emphasis upon professional integrity throughout the organization.

From his first institutional visit, it became clear that every prison must be clean and orderly, that wardens would manage by "walking around" inside the walls and not sitting in offices, and that inmate mistreatment would not be tolerated. These standards began to emerge at his first Wardens' Conference. He told the wardens "We are going to have no more 'house boys,'" referring to inmates who provided services for the warden and his family, and we are going to have no more officers' messes." Several of the older wardens did not like these changes, and they believed that officers' messes gave the officers time to be by themselves and away from inmates.[2]

Dr. Robert Brutsche, a physician who was in charge of the medical services in the Bureau of Prisons, said this about the new director:

> There were several things that were helpful to Norm before he became director.
>
> First, he had gotten into the swing of taking action on a lot of things when he was Myrl Alexander's executive assistant. For example, he had had contact with the wardens.

Second, he had a military style which goes back to Jim Bennett. He was the sort of guy that what he said is the way it was and there were no ifs, ands, or buts.

Third, you are familiar with the 50 and 20 bill about the ability to retire by the age of 55. This idea was to emphasize that corrections was a young man's field. This allowed Norm to get rid of the wardens who had been around for years. When Norm would bring up a subject, they would be the first to complain. Along with that, we began to open new institutions in the 1970s. He began to get more of his wardens into the field.[3]

Mary Rawlings, who had been personal secretary to Myrl Alexander and continued for fifteen years as Norm Carlson's secretary, responded to the question: "Was he a natural leader?"

She said, "I believe that Mr. Carlson had God-given talents to be a leader, and they came out very early. He didn't have any learning curve he had to go through." To the question, "Didn't he stumble a little at first?" she responded, "He didn't stumble or flounder at first. No, not that I am aware. He just went steadily upward. He has a very quick mind. He seems to grasp the situations no matter how difficult they might be. He could just sort out what needed to be done. He made immediate decisions and the right ones."[4]

Challenges of Correctional Administration

John Conrad, a recognized twentieth century student of corrections, said, "Correctional work is not for the faint of heart."[5] Whether you are a correctional officer working in a cellblock, a correctional supervisor, or an administrator of a prison or a corrections system, you would likely agree.

Administrators cannot control prison population numbers. For the Director of the Federal Bureau of Prisons, Congress and the U.S. federal courts would determine how many prisoners were sent to the Bureau of Prisons. As federal prison populations, as well as population of state facilities, began to increase in the 1970s and even more in the 1980s, crowding became a major issue of sometimes crisis proportions. Correctional administrators had no choice but to provide housing for all the inmates.

Inmates, of course, do not want to be in prison. Usually far from home with little or no contact with loved ones, both male and female inmates feel alienated. They must learn to adapt to a world of deprivations, doing without certain comforts and pleasures they enjoyed in the free world. Boredom is ever present. The experienced male or female convict eventually learns to do time but has to fight against going "stir crazy." Furthermore, the total impact of incarceration—one negative experience stacked on the next—hardens a prisoner. Male inmates, especially, learn that the best way to avoid being hurt is to repress their emotions.

Major differences do exist in how male and female prisoners serve their prison sentences. The male must learn to coexist with larger numbers of peers because men's prisons are several times the size of women's prisons. Survival is less certain in men's prisons, so men are more likely to arm themselves for self-protection. In most state and federal prisons, the male prisoner must deal with inmate gangs. Moreover, racial conflict is more acute in men's than in women's prisons. Racial tension sometimes erupts in sexual victimization, in stabbings and killings, and in mass disturbances.

The prison administrator is constantly aware of the possibility of violence in correctional facilities. Prison violence is usually interpreted to mean a prison riot or mass disturbance, but it also means violence of inmates toward each other, toward staff, and staff's violence toward inmates. Prison violence also includes self-inflicted violence when inmates attempt to hurt themselves or may even have successful suicide incidents. Correctional officers are further aware of the dangers present in their jobs, for they daily experience the hostility of inmates. Sometimes they receive verbal abuse; at other times, they are physically assaulted. Officers, too, have been known to retaliate in abusive ways toward inmates.

Furthermore, prior to 1960, it was generally accepted that a convicted individual forfeited all rights not expressly granted by statutory law or correctional policy. Inmates were considered to be civilly dead. As the 1960s drew to a close, the hands-off doctrine was eroded. During this liberal era, Federal courts began to seriously consider prisoners' claims concerning conditions in the various state and federal institutions and used their power to intervene on behalf of the inmates. In some ways, this concern reflected the spirit of the times, which saw the onset of the civil right movement, and subsequently was paralleled in such areas as student rights, mental institutions, juvenile court systems, and military justice.

For correctional administrations, this shift in prisoners' rights meant that they could find themselves in federal court. Proactive administrators, as Norm Carlson turned out to be, attempted to provide constitutionally mandated rights to inmates, but these administrators would still find themselves in court.

The political nature of corrections was another challenge faced by wardens and directors of state systems. When a new governor was elected, it generally meant that there would be a change in the top agency jobs of state government, including the head of the corrections system and often the wardens of correctional facilities. Federal agencies generally also changed when a President of a different political party was elected to the White House. Despite this, the Bureau of Prisons had become a career agency and was able to remain so, though at times there was some question whether the new administration in the White House would appoint a new director.

For these reasons and others, it is not surprising that there was such a high turnover of correctional administrators in the 1970s. In 1979, the author interviewed thirty-six directors or commissioners of state departments of corrections as well as the director of the federal system, Norm Carlson. Three years later, Norm Carlson and a handful of state directors were the only ones still remaining in their jobs.

Finally, Norman Carlson had the disadvantage that he had never served as a warden or even as an associate warden. To make matters even more challenging for him, his background was in treatment, and at the time there was sharp conflict between custody and treatment staff. A good many custody staff questioned whether treatment belonged in prison, and they were reluctant to give treatment staff recognition or credit for anything that went on within a prison. This makes what Norm accomplished during his seventeen years as director of the Federal Bureau of Prisons even more remarkable.

Now, let us examine the problems that he faced during his first decade in office.

Prison Violence

Prison violence was a major issue in American corrections for much of the 1970s. Carlson had been in office for a little over a year when inmates rioted at the Attica State Prison in New York, September 9-13, 1971. In the next four months, violence erupting in prisons across the nation spurred discussion of what could be done to halt it. The U.S. Justice Department, under orders from President Richard Nixon, embarked on a comprehensive, ten-year plan to make the Bureau of Prisons a model for reform. Later, violence at the Federal Correctional Institution Lewisburg culminated in the murder of a number of federal inmates. Director Carlson worried that another murder could cost him his job. He believed "outside agitators" were contributing to the politicization and radical response of some inmates.

Prison Reform as a Means to Halt Prison Violence

In December of 1971, some 300 prison experts throughout the nation gathered in Williamsburg, Virginia, for the First National Conference on Corrections—a meeting called by President Richard Nixon. The President sent a tape-recorded message to the conference, in which he called upon the delegates to "blaze the trail of prison reform." He added: "We have made important strides in the past two years, but let us not deceive ourselves: Our prisons are still colleges of crime, and not what they should be—the beginning of a way back to a productive life within the law."[6]

At the conference, Justice Department officials unveiled a number of plans for spurring prison reform:

- To phase out the nation's large and crowded prisons during a twenty-year period and replace them with smaller, community-oriented institutions. A bill to support this was introduced in Congress, but it was never passed. However, the Bureau of Prisons did embark on a major building program and a number of prisons with exemplary designs were constructed.
- To train prison administrators for federal, state, and local facilities, the Bureau of Prisons opened a training center and established the National Institute of Corrections.
- To discover why criminals violate the law and how they can be stopped or to prevent them from other criminal acts, the Bureau of Prisons was committed to build a national behavioral-research center. This proposal was implemented in the mid-1970s through the design and construction of the Federal Correctional Institution Butner. It was highly influenced by Norval Morris' *The Future of Imprisonment*.[7] Morris was the Dean of the University of Chicago Law School, a personal friend of Carlson, and an informal advisor.
- To help state and local agencies improve their jail facilities, the Law Enforcement Assistant Administration (LEAA) financed a National Clearinghouse for Criminal Justice Architecture at the University of Illinois. This Clearinghouse became operational and for years provided services to local and state agencies.
- To improve educational programs for prisoners, the LEAA funded another clearinghouse—this one on correctional education. At the time, 55 percent of adult felons had only an elementary-school education.
- To reduce racial tensions between prisoners and correctional officers, Attorney General John Mitchell urged prison officials to hire more African Americans and Latino Americans. The Bureau of Prisons set a goal of one-third minority employment in all new hiring. With a strong affirmative stance from Director

Carlson, the Bureau of Prisons never reached this goal but did achieve minority hiring in the high twenties.[8]

LEAA grants to state and local prisons grew from 2 million dollars in the year ending June 30, 1969, to about 250 million in the year ending June 30, 1972. State prison officials used the federal aid to implement changes throughout the nation, including a wide variety of programs—work-release, vocational and educational programs for inmates, probation services for those convicted of misdemeanors, law libraries for inmates, and statewide training programs for employees.

Violence at Lewisburg

One of the major challenges of Norman Carlson's early years was the violence that broke out in the Federal Correctional Institution Lewisburg Penitentiary. Over a period of two years, between March 1974 and May 1976, eight inmates were slain, the highest murder rate of any federal facility. A six-person investigative board examined the conditions and concluded that "The one factor that stands out above all others as a viable explanation for the recent homicides and assaults . . . is the increase in the number of young, aggressive, immature and criminalistic inmates."[9]

The board said it was significant that six murders took place in housing units and five were related to homosexual activity. For example, one victim "was known as a homosexual and a persistent gambler" and "probably was killed for making advances to the homosexual partner of another individual." The board further indicated that the prison staff had failed in a number of ways to exert control over inmates. Top officials permitted poor staff performance, overlooked lax enforcement of regulations, and seldom toured the institution. Some officers were even afraid to patrol dormitories and tended to stay at their desks in the hallway.

Carlson reviewed the board report and knew that something had to be done immediately. He decided to implement the unit management system at this penitentiary (*see* pages 136-137 on unit management), the first time that it had been tried in a penitentiary, and to replace the

Lewisburg warden with Charles Fenton, an experienced and respected federal warden. These strategies seemed to work; there was only one inmate murder at this facility in the next three years.

Outside Agitators and Prison Disturbances

With the increased politicization of inmates, especially in California in the late 1960s, institutional disturbances increased. During the opening day of a national symposium on the American Penal System as a Revolutionary Target (held at the FBI Academy, Quantico, Virginia, June 19-21, 1974) Norm Carlson responded to this issue. A summary of his remarks was published in the *Congressional Record*.

> On the afternoon of opening day, the Symposium was addressed by the Honorable Norman A. Carlson, Director, Federal Bureau of Prisons. Director Carlson noted in his address the problem posed to prison authorities by self-styled "political prisoners," who are influenced by revolutionary groups outside the prison. Director Carlson stated that only a very small percentage of the total inmate population becomes involved with revolutionary groups but this small percentage of prisoners requires a tremendous and disproportionate investment of resource allocation from prison administrators.
>
> In response to this problem, prison administrators, Director Carlson said, should assure that training is afforded correctional staffs so that these staffs will understand what these revolutionary agitators are trying to do. He noted further that prison authorities can always expect criticism. Rather than seeking excuses or placing blame for prison problems on agitators, the courts, or the press, he asked that corrections officials increase contact with the courts, the press, and the public at large, to explain the job and goals of correctional systems. There must also be, Director Carlson said, a willingness to change policies and procedures when deficiencies are found.[10]

In sum, during the 1970s, the Federal Bureau of Prisons had outbursts of violence in several facilities, especially Federal Correctional Institution Lewisburg, but it had nothing like the prison riots at Attica in 1971, San Quentin and Folsom prisons in California during the late 1960s, or at the New Mexico State Prison in Santa Fe in 1980. One proactive strategy of the Bureau during the 1970s was the widespread employment of minority staff members, which will be discussed in a later chapter, and this may have defused somewhat the eruption of collective violence in federal facilities. Director Carlson's actions (cited previously) also suggest that perhaps the attention given the influence of the changing political prisoner on inmate populations was greater than what occurred in some of the state correctional facilities. This may also have been a deterrent against collective violence in federal facilities during the 1970s.

Legal Aspects of Corrections Management

As Director, Carlson oversaw twenty-six federal prisons and some 23,000 inmates in 1970. He tried to visit each of the prisons once a year. He had very strong ideas about what should take place in the institutions: after returning from one of these trips, a staff member told of his displeasure when he found that inmates at one prison had been without napkins for two weeks.

One of Norman Carlson's proactive ways to ensure inmates were granted their First, Fifth, Eighth, and Fourteenth Amendment rights was to invite Al Bronstein, Director of the National Prison Project of the American Civil Liberties Union, to the Bureau of Prisons. They met once a year for a lunch or an afternoon meeting. Bronstein talked about the problems concerning prisoners' rights in both state and federal prisons that he saw as he traveled across the country. He also discussed what he considered were positive and not so positive ways these issues concerning prisoners' rights were handled.[11]

Regardless of Carlson's concern about humane treatment of inmates, the extent and character of their "rights" frequently received the attention of the federal courts and the press. A large number of legal decisions and extremely important constitutional developments occurred during Norm Carlson's tenure. Of the scores of constitutional-issue cases during the 1970s, three cases received particular interest from the press—the question of legitimization of the Church of New Song, the question of whether inmates could publish what they wrote in prison, and the possibility of inmates being interviewed by the press.

The Church of the New Song. The Church of the New Song was founded in 1971 by inmate "Bishop" Harry W. Theriault and other inmates at the Atlanta Federal Penitentiary. In February 1972, U.S. District Court Judge Newell Edenfield startled everyone when he recognized the Church of the New Song as an authentic religious group with the right to practice its beliefs, under the First Amendment, including meeting in space that was given to other religiously sanctioned groups. The self-declared leader, who held a mail-order divinity degree, asked officials of the Atlanta Penitentiary for wine, steak, movies, and medals, which he claimed were needed in the rituals for the 100 recorded members. The special materials requested included almost 100 bottles of Harvey's Bristol Cream sherry, 12 special monthly movies at $75 each, and 200 silver medals with the "Eclatarian" seal. The fund request for $6,000 worth of food, wine, and special materials would permit church members to "sup" with Eclat, the church's supreme entity, a minimum of seven times a year.[12]

"We know that back in the biblical days when people supped, those meals always included wine. Therefore, we cannot invite Eclat to sup with us without having wine and the 'hidden manna,' which we believe is beefsteak since it was a 'hidden' food back then," the request said.

The Church of the New Song also further asked for a $537 IBM Selectric typewriter, $2,249 worth of mimeograph paper, $36 worth of stencils, and $23 worth of correction fluid to reproduce the *Eclatarian Bible* and to publish church bulletins.

About a year later, Judge Edenfield heard new complaints from Theriault. After an extensive hearing, the judge found Norman Carlson and the Reverend Frederick Silber, director of the bureau's chaplaincy services, in contempt of court for violating his 1972 order.

In 1974, the U.S. Fifth Circuit Court of Appeals ruled in favor of Bureau officials whom Theriault had accused of harassment. In its ruling, the Fifth Circuit upbraided Judge Edenfield, saying that his contempt finding was "clearly erroneous and unsupported by the evidence." The appellate court went on: "Upon determining what was intended by the order they complied forthwith (at Atlanta). We are convinced of their complete sincerity and good faith. The contempt finding by the district court (Edenfield) was an abuse of discretion and must be reversed, annulled, and set aside."[13]

However, even after the Fifth Circuit ruling, the Church of the New Song continued to meet at Atlanta. It eventually disappeared, as inmates became bored and stopped attending.[14] Interestingly, Harry Theriault, even though his religious enterprise faded away, continued to write friendly, even personal, letters to Director Carlson for years.

Inmates May Publish. A regulation imposed in 1974 prohibited inmates from attempting to publish materials about their own lives or criminal careers, prison conditions, and prison employees. The 1974 rules further required inmates to get approval from prison officials before attempting to write for publication. The inmate was required to submit an outline of the proposed book or article, and the warden had the power to disapprove it. Manuscripts rejected by the warden were confiscated and not returned to the inmate until the inmate left prison.

The Bureau of Prisons reversed a tradition of censorship in 1976 when Carlson issued an order repealing censorship rules, declaring that it was now the Bureau's policy "to encourage inmates to use their leisure time for creative writing." Carlson's policy statement included cartoons, drawings, music, and lyrics, as well as poetry, fiction, non-fiction articles, and any other writings submitted for publication. Bureau spokesperson, Michael Aun, the public affairs officer, stated that the change was part of a "new trend that the inmate should be permitted to keep up his contacts with his family and the community." "Besides," he stated, "we're just too busy to be censoring manuscripts. It's just not feasible today."[15]

Inmate Interviews with the Press. Norman Carlson, however, resisted for several years granting press interviews with inmates of federal correctional institutions. Ben H. Bagdikian, an assistant managing editor of the *Washington Post* who had written on prison conditions, filed a suit. Bagdikian claimed that the Bureau's blanket refusal to permit in-person interviews with inmates abridged the First Amendment free speech and press rights of prisoners.

Bagdikian's book, *Caged: Eight Prisoners and Their Keepers*, documented the Bureau of Prisons' attempt to prevent him from both corresponding with and especially having face-to-face contact with prisoners. He claimed that some of the prisoners' letters failed to reach him. Some of their letters had been opened, and all of his letters were censored. The inmates involved sued the Bureau of Prisons over the constitutionality of the punishment the prison staff imposed on them.[16]

U.S. District Judge Gerhard A. Gesell in Washington, D.C. agreed with the plaintiffs and ordered the Bureau to issue new interview rules. He also told the Bureau to grant limited access to Bagdikian immediately. This April 5, 1972 ruling by Judge Gesell allowed prison interviews on a case-by-case basis while it was being appealed.[17]

On May 11, 1972, Chief Justice Warren E. Burger temporarily stayed Gesell's order. Solicitor General Erwin N. Griswold informed Burger, on behalf of the Bureau of Prisons, that prisoner hostility and other injury to the prison system could result if they implemented Gesell's order.[18]

Carlson continued to oppose inmate talks with the press. He claimed that the right to interview those inmates who requested it would undermine discipline and endanger prisoners and correctional officers. He told reporters that most inmates who seek interviews are "troublemakers." *The Houston Chronicle* won a suit against the U.S. Attorney General in August 1973, obtaining the right to interview prisoners in federal custody. In that decision, U.S. District Judge John V. Singleton, Jr., ruled that regulations forbidding such interviews constitute "a prior restriction on the press' right to publish, the prisoner's right to speak out and the public's right to know."[19]

The U.S. Supreme Court later reversed the judgment of the appeals court and held that news people have no constitutional right to access prisons or their inmates beyond that afforded the public. This ruling rejected Judges Singleton and Gesell's opinions, and agreed with a decision in a California case that denied news people the right to interview inmates.[20]

In sum, the Carlson administration fared well with the courts during his first decade in office. In interviews, Al Bronstein indicated that he was troubled by only one case in the 1970s and two cases in the 1980s, which are discussed in the next chapter.[21] When you consider the many cases in which the Bureau was involved from 1970-1987, this is a telling testimony to how the Bureau and its legal staff attempted to anticipate and respond to prisoners' rights.

The Changing Role of Rehabilitation

One of the most widely publicized issues in the 1970s was the role of rehabilitation in the Bureau of Prisons. Norm Carlson's thinking gradually evolved from the time he became director in 1970 to the mid-to late-1970s when he began to question the effectiveness of rehabilitation, especially the Medical Model, which implied that criminality, like disease, could be diagnosed and treated. A number of factors influenced Carlson's change of position, concerning the role of rehabilitation in prison.

He was influenced by Robert Martinson's article that "nothing works," published in 1974.[22] This article found that most correctional treatment programs were ineffective. Another influence was that for a number of years, the research department in the Bureau of Prisons had evaluated so-called rehabilitative programs and found that they seemed to have very limited positive results. Findings of the Bureau's Community Treatment Program that were not nearly as positive as he had hoped also influenced him. Finally, "The capstone of my thinking," according to Carlson, was "Norval Morris' book, *The Future of Imprisonment*, which said in effect, 'Look, the problem is you are attempting to force inmates to change; all you can really do is facilitate change and provide opportunities.'"

One of the main propositions of Carlson's belief was that a humane facility allowed rehabilitation programs for those who choose them, but participation should never be forced and should have nothing to do with the length of incarceration.[23] His stance questioning the role of rehabilitation received much criticism from many fronts, especially from officials in state departments of corrections.

By 1975, in a number of interviews and talks, Carlson announced "the end of the Medical Model" at the Bureau of Prisons. In a speech to the annual meeting of the American Academy of Psychiatry and the Law, he noted that the Medical Model did not work and was not needed for the majority of offenders. In its place, he recommended a "Balanced Approach." This Balanced Approach, the theme of his 1980 Presidential address to the American Correctional Association, acknowledged that all four classical goals (rehabilitation, deterrence, incapacitation, and even retribution) are involved when offenders are sent to prison. However, he never said that all four must take place for every offender. His view was that programs, such as education, work, and counseling, are very important to assist those offenders who want to change their behavior.

Carlson further developed this theme of balance in corrections in a speech he delivered at the United Nations Congress on Crime Prevention in Geneva, Switzerland.

> It is quite natural for those of us in corrections, like any other groups of professionals, to try to describe our work in the most positive fashion. . . .
>
> This approach has been helpful in humanizing institutions, but unfortunately, the words employed are medical and mental health terms, which strongly suggest far more expertise than now exists for changing offenders. Such terms foster the belief that we can diagnose offenders as we do people with physical or mental illness, pursue a course of specific treatment, and then bring about a complete cure.

> The hard fact is that we cannot diagnose the cause of crime as we can, for example, trace the source of physical or emotional illness to recognizable diseases such as tuberculosis or schizophrenia. Unfortunately, corrections remains primarily an art and not a science. Consequently, we cannot prescribe with precision the treatment, and it is painfully obvious that we cannot guarantee a cure. . . .
>
> We believe there should be a balanced correctional system—reflecting deterrence and retribution as well as rehabilitation. This should not, however, be interpreted as a return to "the good old days." No responsible criminal justice administrator believes it is desirable to resurrect the barbarous prison conditions of the past; incarceration and the resulting loss of liberty is punishable enough.[24]

In sum, Norm Carlson's position toward rehabilitation became the established position of corrections officials across the nation. Almost all agree that rehabilitation is only one of the goals of corrections. Carlson's theory of the "balance in corrections" is not one that other students of corrections have picked up or espoused. However, the corrections world accepts much of what this theory incorporates.

Prison on Idyllic Lake Placid

Norman Carlson got along well with the media. The issue of placing a prison near Lake Placid at the time of the 1980 Winter Olympics was one of the few events of his first ten years that did generate media criticism.

The 1980 Winter Olympics Games were planned for Lake Placid, New York, and the question was where the funding would come from to build an Olympic Village. Athletes' security had become a major issue since the murders of Israeli athletes at the 1972 Summer Olympics in Munich, Germany.

Congressman Robert C. McEwen approached President Gerald Ford to fund the building of the Olympic Village, but the main issue

57

was whether there would be sufficient perimeter security. President Ford agreed that the federal government would provide the funds, but added that it had to have a secondary use. McEwen went to Congressman Robert Slack, the chair of the House Appropriations Subcommittee that handled the budget for the Department of Justice, and said that he had the approval of the President if the Olympic Village had a further later use. McEwen proposed to build dormitory facilities to house some 1,800 athletes for the 1980 Winter Olympics. Thereafter, the "Olympic Village" would become the newest federal prison. The federal government was paying the entire $22 million cost of the facility, including its post-Olympic conversion from housing to prison.[25]

The local Olympic planners were, of course, pleased. The people of Lake Placid, according to Representative McEwen who represented the Adirondack district, were also pleased. With the highest unemployment rate in the state of New York, they welcomed the prospect of more than 200 prison jobs at an average pay of $15,000. The Bureau of Prisons, while acknowledging the site ran somewhat counter to its own guidelines, considered the Olympic Village-turned prison a good deal.[26]

On the other side were groups that considered this a wrong move by the federal government. As one newspaper article put it, "a devious move by elements of our federal government threatens to garnish Lake Placid's signal honor, spoil the spirit of camaraderie and sportsmanship associated with the Olympics, and turn a potentially beautiful Olympic 'village' into a day concentration camp."[27] However, the village was built and it continues as part of the Bureau of Prisons.

Crisis of the Body Crunch

In testimony before the Subcommittee on Penitentiaries and Corrections of the Senate Committee on the Judiciary in January 1978, Norman Carlson reflected on the problem of crowding in prisons, a concern of all correctional administrators in the late 1970s and 1980s:

> If you were to visit any of our (federal) institutions, the first thing you would observe is severe overcrowding. To be candid, the major problem facing most prison administrators today in this country is 'The Body Crunch,' the pressure of a rapidly increasing inmate population. The population problem can be summed up in one sentence: more offenders being committed to institutions for longer terms and for more aggressive and assaultive crimes. . . . Despite the fact that the Federal Prison System has acquired or built nine new institutions in the past six years, which has added space for 3,800 offenders to our physical capacity, we have more than 30,400 inmates today in space designed for less than 23,000.[28]

The magnitude of this problem was such that it appeared in newspapers covering Carlson's speeches and interviews through the remainder of the years that he served as director of the Bureau of Prisons. To handle this "body crunch," the Bureau constructed several new prisons during the 1970s.

Conclusions

This chapter considered a number of the newsworthy issues that took place from the time that Norm Carlson became director in 1970 through 1979. The most significant of these events was the relative lack of violence, especially collective violence in the Federal Bureau of Prisons. The Bureau of Prisons did not have any riots like that of Attica, San Quentin, or Soledad. Norm Carlson did receive a barrage of criticism with his position on rehabilitation, but in the end, his position became widely accepted in the corrections world. The press criticised the Bureau of Prisons and its director, Norman Carlson. Yet, Carlson's policy of being open to the media and responding to reporters' questions obviously contributed to the largely positive presentation he received from them. In addition, as suggested throughout this text, the Bureau of Prisons as a standard-setter simply did not merit the negative press that some state departments of corrections received.

Endnotes

1. Kathleen Hawk Sawyer sent this letter to the author on August 28, 2005.

2. Carlson's interview was in July 2005.

3. Robert Brutsche, Ph.D., was interviewed September 2005.

4. Mary Rawlings was interviewed September 2005.

5. He made this statement to the author a number of times while we were working on a corrections project together.

6. Norm Carlson in July 2000 reported this to the author.

7. Norval Morris. 1974. *The Future of Imprisonment*. Chicago: University of Chicago Press.

8. 1971. "Drive to Halt Prison Violence." *U. S. News and World Report*, December 27.

9. Report is in the archives of the Federal Bureau of Prisons, Washington, D.C.

10. 1974. *Congressional Record—Extensions of Remarks*, July 29.

11. Alvin Bronstein was interviewed June 2008.

12. 1972. "Prison Sect: 'Send Us Wine, Not Rosaries.'" *Dallas Times Herald*, May 28.

13. 1974. "Court Rules Against Prison Church Here." *The Atlanta Constitution*, June 13.

14. Correspondence from the warden of Atlanta at the time.

15. 1976. "Inmates May Publish: Censorship Reversed." *Petersburg, Virginia Progress*, April 1.

16. Ben H. Bagdikian. 1976. *Caged: Eight Prisoners and Their Keepers*. New York: Harper and Row, Publishers.

17. U.S. District Court for the District of Columbia, *The Washington Post Co. v. Kleindienst*, 357 F. Supp. 770 (1972).

18. U.S. District Court for the District of Columbia, *The Washington Post Co. v. Kleindienst*, 357 F. Supp. 779 (1972).

19. U.S. District Court for the Southern District of Texas, Houston Division, *Houston Chronicle Publishing Company v. Kleindienst*, 364 F. Supp. 719 (1973).

20. U.S. Supreme Court, *Saxbe, Attorney General v. Washington Post Co.*, 417 U.S. 843, 94 S. Ct. 2811m 41 K, Ed. 2d 514 (1974).

21. Interviewed June 2008.

22. Robert Martinson. 1974. "What Works?:—Questions and Answers About Prison Reform." *Public Interest 35*, Spring, pp. 22-54.

23. Norval Morris. 1974. *The Future of Imprisonment*. Chicago: The University of Chicago Press.

24. 1975. "A Balance in Corrections." *Minneapolis Star*, October 1.

25. William Raspberry. 1978. "From Olympic Dormitory to Prison: Bad Idea?" *Washington Post*, Washington, D.C., July 28.

26. Ibid.

27. William Rentschler. 1979. "Prison Plan Spoils Lake Placid Games." *Chicago Tribune*, July 15.

28. 1978. "Carlson Cites 'Body Crunch' as Major Problem: Testimony Before Senate Committee." *Correctional News*, January.

Chapter 5
Leadership in the 1980s

He always saw THE BIG PICTURE as to what was going on. Not just in the BOP, but within corrections overall. Also, he worked hard on his relationships within the Department of Justice, the Bureau of the Budget, Congress, the Courts, the U.S. Marshals, etc. He was good from the beginning and got better.

He is an imposing figure who was always well versed on the topics he spoke to. He not only looked the part of a leader, when he spoke, he sounded like a leader. He didn't waste time trying to impress you with any flowery talk. He spoke to the issues, made good sense and the results provide his leadership qualities.

Roy Gerard, Assistant to the Director[1]

Carlson's final eight years as director, from 1980 to 1987, were every bit as eventful as his first decade in office. Media coverage was much the same, but in the early 1980s, it focused on the violence at the U.S. Penitentiary in Marion, Illinois. Murders and assaults at Marion included the deaths of two correctional officers and the wounding of several others on the same day in October 1983. In another case, shots were fired into the homes of Carlson and an assistant.

During this era, Chief Justice Burger emphasized the importance of teaching inmates a trade. Castro opened Cuba's mental hospitals and prisons, and deported their inhabitants and other misfits, leading to the problem of incarcerating Cuban offenders. Corruption among the custodial staff at the Terminal Island prison in California, and a few controversial court cases rounded out the media's attention.

The theme of treatment was largely ignored in the 1980s. However, a new psychiatric hospital was added to the Bureau of Prisons, but the context of the times was that of law and order. Those fostering treatment options received little support.

Violence at Marion, Illinois

One of the most widely publicized events in corrections in the 1980s was the murder of two officers in the Federal Penitentiary in Marion, Illinois. The incident began on Saturday morning, October 22, 1983, when an inmate fatally stabbed Merle Eugene Clutts, fifty-one, a senior officer specialist, in a cell area of the H unit, a control unit apart from the general prison population. He was pronounced dead on arrival at the Marion Memorial Hospital. Ten hours later, Robert L. Hoffman Sr., fifty-three, was also pronounced dead on arrival at the Marion Hospital. Also wounded in the attack on Hoffman Saturday night were correctional officers Jerry L. Powles, thirty-five, and Roger D. Ditterline, thirty.[2]

The first attack occurred as three correctional officers escorted inmate Thomas Silverstein, thirty, in handcuffs from the showers to his cell. Without warning, the strapping "very strong, very aggressive" inmate paused in the hall of his cell block outside another prisoner's cell. When he turned around, his hands were free and he was holding a razor-sharp, eighteen-inch knife fashioned from a sharpened bedspring.[3] Silverstein struggled with the correctional officers, pinning officer Clutts against the wall and stabbing him in the chest. Before the other officers could subdue him, Clutts, a grandfather and a well-respected prison veteran who was to retire the next May, was dead.

The second event took place after 8 p.m. the same day, as four officers escorted Clayton Fountain, twenty-eight, in handcuffs to his cell from the recreational area. The attack was sickeningly familiar to the first one. The inmate paused outside another prisoner's cell, pulled out a long, handmade knife and, with his hands free, began to swing it at the officers. In the battle Hoffman found himself in relative safety near the exit door of the cell block. However, he refused to abandon his fellow officers and jumped back into the fray. Minutes later he was stabbed to death. Two other officers, Powles and Ditterline, were later hospitalized with knife wounds, but they were in stable condition by the next day.[4]

Marion was known to house the federal system's most violent, escape-prone inmates. Since this penitentiary was opened in 1964, twenty-five inmates and three correctional officers, including the two on that grim October Saturday in 1983, were murdered and fifty-eight inmates and twenty-seven correctional officers were assaulted with weapons. On October 27, the next week after the fatal stabbings of the two officers, an inmate, Jack B. Callison, forty-one, was found stabbed to death in his cell.[5]

Three further newsworthy events occurred subsequent to the murders at the Marion facility. The first related to allegations of beatings at Marion. Attorneys met with the Marion Warden, Jerry Williford, and said that they would file a class action suit in U.S. District Court on behalf of sixteen Marion inmates. The attorneys claimed that prison officials exhibited a "continuing pattern of brutality, abuse and deprivation of constitutional rights" and said that they would also seek monetary damages for the prisoners but did not specify the amount. It was claimed that the strategy of prison officials was "to terrorize and humiliate the prisoners and strip them of any shred of dignity." The federal courts, however, after hearing the evidence, dismissed all charges of brutality of correctional officers toward inmates.[6]

The second event was the court action taken from the extended lockdown of inmates at Marion. This court action was filed in the local federal court, which upheld the use of long-term, near-total lockdown of prisoners at the out-of-control federal prison at Marion, Illinois.[7] A federal appeals court upheld this decision.[8] The importance of this decision was that it resulted in the spread of supermax facilities across the nation, in which prisoners could be placed in twenty-four hour lockdown for extended periods of time.

Another consequence of the violence at Marion was the mounting support for a bill in Congress that supported the death penalty for federal inmates who kill staff or other inmates while in prison.

Exhibit 4.1 is a statement Norman A. Carlson gave to the Criminal Law Subcommittee of the U.S. Senate Judiciary Committee in support of S. 1765, which proposed to restore the death penalty in the federal system. This bill became law.

Exhibit 4.1 Statement of Norman Carlson on the Death Penalty for Those Killing Federal Officers

"Those incidents [at Marion] dramatically illustrate the problems we have in attempting to cope with criminals for whom there is no meaningful deterrent. In my opinion, the lack of a federal death penalty makes a mockery of the Federal Criminal Justice System when we attempt to deal with multiple murderers who continue to prey on innocent victims, both staff and inmates.

"Recent events at Marion have been a tragic experience—not only for the families involved and the slain officers' friends and co-workers, but for all of us in federal law enforcement. What could make these tragedies even more appalling would be a determination that those responsible were already serving life sentences and are in effect immune from any further sanction for their acts.

"Where assailants are already serving multiple consecutive life sentences, they can act with impunity since a life sentence is the most severe penalty that the Federal Criminal Justice System presently authorizes as punishment for murder. One more life sentence means absolutely nothing to them.

"Without debating the arguments justifying the various theories of criminal sanctions—retribution, deterrence, or incapacitation—individuals serving life sentences are immune from further punishment. Repeated, barbaric acts against both staff and inmates demonstrate that they are not deterred from further violence. Another life sentence adds nothing to the scales of justice. They are already incapacitated to the maximum extent which our system allows. . . . We in the Criminal Justice System are powerless to act. It is they who choose to execute others while society remains silent.

"I believe that society can demand the death penalty for the repeated taking of human lives. The tragic murders of the correctional officers at Marion dramatically illustrate the need for that ultimate sanction."

Source: *On the Line*, January 1984.

In sum, the murders of staff at the Marion Federal Penitentiary had quite an effect on the Bureau of Prisons. It gave rise to the supermax prison, first in the Bureau at Marion and later in state correctional systems, across the nation. This violence also contributed to Congress restoring the death penalty for federal crimes, including the taking of staff and inmate's lives in federal facilities.

Chief Justice Pushes Jobs For Inmates

Chief Justice Warren E. Burger repeatedly expressed his commitment to improve conditions in the tense and crowded U.S. prisons. Chief Justice Burger was a close personal friend of Director James V. Bennett, a friendship that developed when Burger served as an Assistant Attorney General in the Department of Justice and continued while he was on the Circuit Court of Appeals in Washington, D.C. Many of Burger's ideas, as well as his interest in prisons, appeared to come from this relationship with Bennett.[9] Burger had also studied prisons in Europe, the Soviet Union, and China.

Burger's top goal was to let inmates make goods for sale outside prison walls.[10] Burger's most widely held concern was turning prisons into "factories with fences." In a conference on how this could be done, Burger said, "The key to every good system . . . is work, work, work, along with education and vocational training." Another widely quoted saying is: "To put people behind walls and bars and do little or nothing to change them is to win a battle but lose a war. It is wrong. It is expensive. It is stupid."[11]

The Bureau of Prisons had long placed an emphasis on prison industries. Federal Prison Industries (FPI) was established as "a wholly owned, non-appropriated government corporation, created by Congress in 1934 to sell solely to the government. Its goods are marketed under the trade name UNICOR." This prison program managed by correctional professionals was "created to provide work for inmates, instill a work ethic in individuals with little past work experience or training, and teach inmates skills so that they will be better prepared to return to the community."[12] In 1989, shortly after Norman Carlson's 1987 retirement, more than 14,000 inmates were employed by Federal Prison Industries, and its 1989 sales were approximately $360 million.[13]

Incarceration of Deported Cubans

When Cuba opened its jails and mental institutions and foisted thousands of refugees with criminal records on the United States during the Mariel boatlift of 1980, some ended up seriously damaging the U.S. Penitentiary in Atlanta, Georgia and the Federal Detention Center in Oakdale, Louisiana. Interestingly, the inmates were protesting because they did not want to be returned to Cuba. However, officials came to the conclusion that the Cubans who were housed at the Atlanta Penitentiary, in the words of Norman Carlson, "are among the most violent and dangerous that I have come in contact with during my twenty-five years in prison administration."[14]

The United States wanted to return criminals to Cuba, but in a four-year lawsuit, inmates charged that they would be persecuted if they were sent back to Cuba. They eventually lost this suit, and many were returned to Cuba.[15] Copies of a neatly typed letter were handed to inmates at the Atlanta Federal Penitentiary. The letter informed inmates in Spanish that they were being sent back to their homeland, Cuba. Each inmate received a cardboard box to pack whatever belongings he had when he came to the prison and anything he had managed to obtain while he was there, as long as it was not a weapon or illegal contraband. The deportation list of some 2,700 names was drawn up by U.S. officials and accepted by Cuba.[16]

Not long after Norman Carlson retired, the Cuban prisoners ended up torching the Federal Atlanta Penitentiary and a Federal Detention Center in Oakdale, Louisiana, the worst mayhem in federal prison history.

Shooting at the Homes of the Director and his Assistant

In 1980, while Norman Carlson and his executive assistant, James A. Meko, and their families were attending the American Correctional Association Congress of Correction in San Diego, California, between August 14th and 19th, bullets were fired into their homes. One bullet shattered a front window, a second lodged above the front door, and the third cracked a ground-floor wall in Carlson's home. Meko described the bullet holes at his house as "pencil-sized," and said "that two passed the length of his living room and lodged in a back wall, a third penetrated his front door, grazing the ceiling, and the fourth was found below a bay window."[17]

When the incidents occurred, sources in the FBI and the Department of Justice speculated that the attack may have been in retaliation for the imprisonment of Iranian protesters at the Federal Correctional Institution at Otisville, New York and the Federal Metropolitan Correctional Center in New York City. The Department of Justice sources pointed out that the shootings took place less than two weeks after 191 Iranian demonstrators, arrested after violent clashes with District of Columbia police July 27, were released from federal facilities.[18]

In April of 1981, a federal grand jury in Alexandria indicted a thirty-one year-old Washington, D.C. man on charges that he fired gunshots into the homes of Carlson and his assistant. A four-count indictment was filed against Melvin Lee Davis, also known by his Muslim name, Muhammad Abdul Malik. The indictment charged that Davis and others known to the grand jury conspired to injure Carlson, Meko, and the assistant director of the Bureau of Prisons, Gary R. Mote. Law enforcement officials said that Mote was also a target of the alleged conspiracy although no specific action was carried out against him.[19]

Corrupt Correctional Officers at Terminal Island

One of the ugly pages in the history of the Bureau of Prisons was the 1980s corruption among correctional officers at the federal facility at Terminal Island, California. Four prison employees were indicted, another fourteen prison officials were fired or resigned, four others were disciplined, and four were transferred to other federal prisons.[20]

One fired correctional officer was sentenced to fifteen years in prison for selling marijuana to inmates and helping two of them escape. U.S. District Court Judge Malcolm M. Lucas said, "The only difference between him and the inmates who testified at the trial was that the inmates had already admitted what they had done and were being punished for it." He added that this officer lied when he took the stand in his own defense. At his trial, the officer described himself as a kindhearted officer who took a special interest in inmates, even to the point of trying to find employment for one. He denied selling marijuana and said he did not help two inmates escape in November 1981.[21]

According to testimony given at the trial, this officer had opened a prison gate for the two inmates and had them driven off in his pickup truck. He charged $25,000 for the service. The driver was not caught. One escapee, a convicted heroin dealer, remains at large. The officer was also convicted of selling thousands of dollars worth of marijuana to inmates.[22]

Two former officials, whose responsibility included inmate discipline and the supervision of other officers, pled guilty to five charges involving accepting bribes and stealing money from inmates. A fourth former officer was sentenced to five years for selling drugs in the prison.[23]

While this is an egregious example of corruption in the Federal Bureau of Prisons, a future chapter will tell of Norm Carlson's efforts to create an agency within the Bureau to reduce corruption and to avoid such unacceptable behaviors from taking place.

New Psychiatric Hospital for the Bureau of Prisons

The late Dr. Ruth Westrick Connolly, a psychiatrist in private practice in Rochester, Minnesota, related a conversation she had with Warren Burger, former Supreme Court Chief Justice:

> I was having lunch one day with Warren Burger, former Supreme Court Chief Justice and Associate Justice, Harry Blackman, when I mentioned that the Minnesota State Hospital had been closed. I indicated that there were thirteen buildings and forty acres of ground, and the Mayo Clinic was not interested in buying or utilizing it. Later, Chief Justice Burger and Norm Carlson were having lunch, and Norm said to Chief Justice Burger that it was very difficult to employ good physicians, because they do not like to work in prison systems. Chief Justice Burger informed Norm that the facilities of the former state hospital at Rochester were available. He told Norm that he also had been told that the Mayo Clinic had agreed to be available and helpful. Burger called me and said that Norm was coming to Rochester to see what we have here.[24]

As soon as the Rochester community found out that the Bureau of Prisons might be interested, a strong reaction and controversy led to suits attempting to stop the Bureau. Based on prior experience with the Olympic Village, authorities knew they needed to act swiftly. The Bureau of Prisons bought a portion of the former Rochester State Hospital to convert it into a prison hospital. Bureau officials handed a check for $14 million to Olmsted County Board members and received the deed to the property. The exchange in the county board room occurred only minutes after Congress had approved the Bureau's funding request.[25]

Dr. Westrick Connolly described the final chapter of this site controversy in Rochester between the Bureau and the town. She said:

There was a strong but vocal minority who questioned why Rochester should become a prison town. It led to a legal confrontation. The Bureau of Prisons initially won in court, and when it was appealed, the Eighth Circuit [Court of Appeals] refused to reverse the decision. Once the Bureau came, it was received with open arms. What also improved the reception was that the employment was down at the time for Rochester. There was a picture in the paper of 3,000 people lined up for job interviews to see if there would be employment possibilities with the Bureau of Prisons.[26]

Conclusions

In the last eight years of Norman Carlson's tenure, news events affected the Bureau of Prisons' penal policy. This was especially true with the violence at the Marion Penitentiary. What transpired was an extended lockdown of inmates, which was litigated and sustained in federal court. Marion was permitted to remain in locked-down status, and other "supermax" prisons, as they came to be called, followed in thirty-six states. The violence at Marion also resulted in the return of the death penalty in the federal prison system. Burger's "factories with fences" concept received a great deal of fanfare, but had very little effect on long-term policy. Corruption at Terminal Island, California, revealed that even with the establishment of an Internal Affairs Unit in the Bureau of Prisons and a continued emphasis on integrity, corruption can remain a problem for advanced prison systems.

Endnotes

1. Roy Gerard was interviewed August 2005.

2. 1983. "Two prison guards killed in stabbings," *The Marion Daily Republican*, October 24.

3. 1983. "2 racists suspected in prison deaths." *Chicago Tribune*, October 30.

4. Ibid.

5. Lynn Emmerman. 1983. "Crackdown follows 3 killings at Marion," *Chicago Tribune*, November 8.

6. "Allegations of beatings at Marion prison dismissed." 1984. *Marion Daily Republican*, June 29.

7. *Brucino v. Carlson*, (Civil Action, No. 84-4320), D.C.S.D. Ill (1987).

8. On July 22, 1988, the U.S. Court of Appeals for the Seventh Circuit affirmed *Brucino*.

9. Ibid.

10. Gail S. Funke, ed. 1986. *National Conference on Prison Industries: Discussion and Recommendations*, Washington, D.C.: National Center for Innovation in Corrections.

11. Ibid.

12. Richard P. Seiter. 1990. "Federal Prison Industries: Meeting the Challenge of Growth," *Federal Prisons Journal 1*, Spring, p. 11.

13. Ibid.

14. Ibid.

15. Bob Dart and Andy Ryan. 1988. "Justice Department: Cuban Detainee Bill Sets Cubans Free. *The Atlanta Journal* and *The Atlanta Constitution*. July 7.

16. Monte Plott. 1985. "Atlanta prison is staging area for deportees." *The Atlanta Constitution*, February 28.

17. Ibid.

18. Christopher P. Winner and Micael Isikoff. 1980. "Iranian Angle Probed in Shooting at Home of U.S. Prisons Chief." *Fairfax Star*, September 11.

19. Ibid.

20. Suzanne Bilello. 1981. "Man Indicted in Plot to Harm Prison Chief, *Washington Star*, April 9.

21. Dan Morain. 1983. "Guard Who Aided Escapees Sentenced." *Los Angeles Times*, June 21.

22. Ibid.

23. Ibid.

24. Dr. Ruth Westrick Connolly was interviewed September 2005.

25. Bill McAuliffe. 1984. "Part of Rochester State Hospital Purchased by Bureau of Prisons," *The Denver Post*. Tuesday, May 26.

26. Dr. Ruth Westrick Connolly was interviewed September 2005.

Chapter 6

Post-Retirement Years

I was just with him in Las Vegas [2005] and you know that he hasn't aged. He still looks like he just came from the farm in Sioux City, Iowa. It is utterly charming.

Steve Grzegorek, former Regional Director and Warden[1]

I always admired his very simple, non-egotistical, Midwestern upbringing sort of approach. When I heard that he was retiring, it was like your father was quitting work. He was all that most of us ever knew as Director.

Steve Schwalb, former Warden, Chief of the Internal Affairs Unit, and Assistant Director of the Bureau of Prisons[2]

More than one interviewee talked about the sadness of seeing Norm pack up his belongings and leave the agency on that final day. Staff throughout the Bureau expressed genuine regret at the departure of someone who had guided their agency so well.

Norm may have aged well, but much has taken place in his life in the more than twenty-three years since he retired in 1987. There has been death. In 1994, Pat Carlson, his wife, succumbed to cancer after a few months' fight. They had a loving, close and supportive relationship, going all the way back to college, and it was a hard loss. Friends who knew Norm talked about how he grieved for his beautiful wife. During his early years of his retirement, Norm also lost his mother and father, and in 2003 his only sibling, a sister, died.

Norm also has much joy, however, from his two children, Gary and Cindy, who are happily married, one in Minnesota and the other in Lake Tahoe, California. They both work in public administration, and Norm is pleased with their professional accomplishments. Norm and his second wife, Phyllis, go to visit Norm's children and three grandsons on a regular basis.

Norm led a busy professional life after retiring from the Bureau of Prisons. For the first ten years, he taught at the University of Minnesota, first in the Humphrey Institute and then in the Department of Sociology. He also served as a consultant in Hawaii, Utah, Illinois, and Arizona. In addition, he served as a special master for the U.S. District Court in Maryland in connection with the Baltimore City Jail and as a special monitor for the Federal Court in New York City in a case involving Rikers Island Jail. He has continued to serve on the National Institute of Corrections' Advisory Board, including two years as chairman, and is also the chair of the Past President's Council of the American Correctional Association. For the past ten years, he has been a member of the Board of Directors of The GEO Group, the second largest private correctional organization in the world.

University Teaching

David Ward, Ph.D., recalled Norm's decision to become a university teacher. Norm and David, whose relationship extends back to the late 1950s, had discussed teaching for some time. In 1983 when Ward was a visiting professor at the law school in Berkeley, he asked Norm to speak to two of his classes. Ward related:

> Being the smart guy he is, Norm brought an African-American Bureau staff member with him. He wanted to be certain that a 6'4" straight-looking guy with a crew cut would be accepted on a university campus, like Berkeley with its long history of liberal stances. What he found were students who were interested in criminal policy and sympathetic about locking up bad guys. It was kind of a revelation to him that he could go to a university campus and not have his views attacked by the students.[3]

Chapter 6 - Post-Retirement Years

David Ward returned to the University of Minnesota where he was chairperson of the sociology department. The conversations between Ward and Carlson continued, and immediately following Norm's retirement, Norm began a teaching position at the University of Minnesota.

Pat and he wanted to build a home in Minnesota. They purchased property and built a lovely home in Stillwater, a short distance from St. Paul, the twin city to Minneapolis, and not far from the University of Minnesota campus. Their son, Gary, and his family also lived in Minneapolis. It seemed to the Carlsons an ideal place to live and work for the years to come.

Norm's initial appointment appeared to be a good fit for the Hubert Humphrey Institute of Public Affairs at the university. Norm had all of the Washington D.C. connections. He could place students as interns in many government agencies. "He had," David Ward put it, "been everywhere and had done everything."[4] But the problem in the Humphrey Institute was "that he encountered faculty members who were threatened by someone teaching in the area of public administration who had actually done it."[5]

When it became clear that this arrangement was not working out very well, Ward offered Norm a teaching position in the Department of Sociology, where he taught a couple of courses each semester, including a large Introduction to Criminal Justice course. This worked very well, and Norm taught for ten years at the University of Minnesota.

How did the students like him? What impact did he have on their lives and future careers? In Exhibit 6.1, David Ward, Ph.D., responds to these questions and later in this section, Michael Massoglia, Ph.D., one of Norm's students, reveals the impact Norman Carlson had on his career.

Exhibit 6.1 Students' Response to Norman A. Carlson as a Classroom Teacher

"I think initially his presence in the classroom, and I think that would be true for any of us, who do something completely new, was a little stiff. First of all, he doesn't look like a professor—big and a crew cut. Second, he had spent his whole career learning to be constrained when he talked publicly—to keep things simple because the more you tell the House Subcommittees, the more they might go after you. The same was true with the press.

"It took him a while to loosen up. I remember telling him, 'Students need to hear some stories. You have been through many, many things that students will find interesting.'

"What gradually happened is that students who came around to talk with him found that he was tremendously available and helpful and a very nice person. I think part of the problem for any of us is that teaching at the big university with 200 students out there in a lecture hall makes us question how we can reach individual students.

"I think that Norm's university experience was helpful in that it gave him something valuable to do and allowed him to carry on his consulting activity. He was a special master at Rikers Island for Rudy Giuliani, and he was also able to take on other cases that interested him.

"I was chair of the Sociology Department for a number of years when Norm was there, and we required student evaluations of every course. He got tremendous evaluation scores—really outstanding. He started out with good scores and got even better as time went on. He was very big for bringing in people who were working in the field from the outside, and students always liked that.

"There were dozens of times that I asked Norm to talk to my classes. I have heard his lecture dozens and dozens of times, but I think the best measure of his teaching effectiveness were those student evaluations. Students saw him as one of those exceptional faculty members who was the real deal. He had been out in the real world and knew everybody in the Department of Justice and corrections. Students recognized and appreciated his expertise and his experience.

"Norm's relationship with students tells us that while he might have been feared by wardens, he was a sensitive man when dealing with those further down the chain of command."

Source: David Ward, Ph.D., was interviewed March 2008.

Several interviewees, who have taught on the college level, worked with Norm, and had heard him speaking on the Hill and with Bureau staff, have questioned how effective Norm would be as a classroom teacher. As Professor Ward noted, he began a little stiff, and his style was not similar to those instructors whose flamboyance attract a large student following. Yet, Norm brought three attributes to the position that elicited an extremely positive response at the University of Minnesota.

First, students respected his background and experience, and appreciated the quality of outside speakers that he brought to his classes. Second, he was also more than willing to talk to students when they came around to see him, and his counsel and direction were quite helpful, particularly to students who wanted the experience of spending a term or a summer internship in criminal justice agencies. Finally, demonstrating his quick learning curve, that proved so critical to him during his early years as director of the Bureau of Prisons, he "loosened up" his classroom presence and became an outstanding teacher to hundreds of University of Minnesota students.

During Norm's years at the University of Minnesota, one of the older graduate students, Will Alexander, approached the chair of the department, Professor Ward, about being assigned as Norm's teaching assistant. Will had served time on drug charges in federal prison during Norm's tenure as director and was cautious about Norm's reaction. Yet, as Ward expected when he broached the subject, Norm readily agreed. For the next term and several others, a group of University of Minnesota students had the unique experience of learning about prisons from the man who ran them and from one of the men who was confined in them. Norm's course with Will got the highest student evaluations in the department.

Norm understood that participating in this unusual relationship meant a great deal to a former prisoner working to straighten out his life. Will recently passed away, but he liked to talk about the warm, friendly, and accepting manner in which Norm took him on as an assistant. While doing time as a prisoner, Will Alexander never imagined that one day he would be involved in a joint venture with the head of the federal prison system.

In Exhibit 6.2, Michael Massoglia, Ph.D., who was one of Carlson's students, reveals what impact Norm had on his career:

Exhibit 6.2 My Relationship with Norman Carlson

"It was about 1994 when I was an undergraduate student at the University of Minnesota that I had Norman Carlson for a class in corrections. We developed a friendship in that class, which was very professor-student related. He wrote me letters of recommendations. He offered me a lot of feedback on ideas that I had. I was interested then in the impact that prisons had on people's lives. And he was tremendously influential in my decision to go to graduate school. Over the course of two or three years, I probably took four classes from him. And I bet we would talk once every other week or at least once every three weeks. I would come and we would chat about what he saw and what he experienced. He would tell me what he thought the role of incarceration was, and we would discuss the expansion in the system that started in the early 1970s.

As I got closer to going to graduate school, he helped me look at schools. He helped and guided me in places that he thought would be beneficial to me. He was a tremendous mentor.

In addition to graduate school mentoring, he got me set up for a summer internship in the National Institute of Corrections. He made a call to the director out there, and a week later I got a call from the director to come out for an informal interview. I flew out, and they offered me a job.

I came back to the University of Minnesota, finished up my undergraduate work, and Norm was my faculty advisor for my last year there. I went to graduate school, and we kept in contact. I would send him an e-mail or call from time to time. I came back to the University of Minnesota the same year he retired. I got my M.A. at Washington State.

We probably didn't talk for a year or two. It took me a year to formulate my dissertation, which was the effect of incarceration on health. I started going back to Norm, and he would offer me insights based on his experience that I built into my dissertation. More recently, I am working with him to try to get access to the inmate population for surveys.

It is hard for me to think of my academic career, without thinking of the influence Norm had, either directly or indirectly. I got my Ph.D. from the University of Minnesota. I came to Penn State and have been here about eighteen months as an assistant professor."

Source: Michael Massoglia, Ph.D., was interviewed April 2007.

Norman Carlson is an artist in many areas. Even in teaching, not a natural vehicle of expression for him, he used his skills and resources, evolving over the years. Students responded well, and by the end of his ten years at the University of Minnesota, he had become an excellent teacher, perhaps even a "Master Teacher," a description of a top-notch teacher that is sometimes used in university circles.

David Ward did add two sad notes to his excellent ten-year career. "I think what was most annoying to me was the failure of the Humphrey Institute to take advantage of his expertise. That is what happens when you are so much better than the local people who see you as a threat."[7] He further said: "I was also disappointed that the Minnesota Department of Corrections did not take advantage of Norm's expertise and background when he was right there in the neighborhood. However, he did know that things were not going wrong in Minnesota prisons, and he was not needed there as much as he was in other states, such as his work for the legislature in Hawaii—a Department of Corrections in trouble with a federal judge."[8]

Consulting

Norm may have had to grow into becoming a stellar teacher, but consulting was natural to him. He felt comfortable in examining the principles of the cases at hand. In Exhibit 6.3, Steve Martin, who represented the other side of the table in the *Sheppard, et al. v. Phoenix et al.* case (a class action suit brought by the Legal Aid Society involving conditions and procedures in the Central Punitive Segregation Unit on Riker's Island) described the tremendous respect he has for Norm's skills in the consulting arena.[9]

Exhibit 6.3 You Better Bring Your Best Game to the Table

"Norm is the type of individual that through discourse and discussion forces those around him to be able to articulate and to develop sound rationale and reason for whatever the issue is. He is the type who stays somewhat neutral and does not show his cards until there is a reason to do so. After everything has bubbled up, his position will begin to emerge. In instances where reasonable minds differ, he never took real strong positions. You would know where he would stand, but you'll also know that he was open to discussing things further, new facts, and so forth.

"He has a foundation of principles, and if you hit on one of those principles he feels strongly about, he will voice an equally strong opinion. He doesn't stake out positions on every issue. He is very adept and adaptive. If he takes a strong position, it forces people like me to think their positions through because he is very selective. He doesn't make pronouncements.

"He would say, 'Let's think about this. Have you looked at that? Should we look at that?'

"He has a very inquiring mindset. I have to believe this is one of the reasons he was so effective so long in the Bureau.

"He is very, very crafty. You know it is not just his assets or his ability to maneuver. It is grounded in sound principles. He is a good corrections guy, first and foremost, but he happens to have these other skills. He is really a total management package. There aren't that many in our field that have anywhere near his skill level.

"I think Norm is extremely sensitive to the issue of credibility. He is very protective of his credibility. I can recall we used to meet with the presiding judge of the *Sheppard* case, Judge Patterson. Norm would attend these meetings, and, for the most part, would listen. He really wouldn't interject his opinion, unless he thought his credibility would advance or resolve a particular issue. So, he was always very constructive.

"Norm was quite skillful in allowing people to state their views. He would pull something out of an opposition view, in identifying some part of that, which he can use as a bridge to bring that into the fold.

"At any point in time in which you are dealing with him, you better bring your best game to the table. I always took great pride in being able to monitor that case with him. I wanted to do my absolute best in working with him. He brings out the best in people."

Source: Interviewed October 2005.

David Ward, a frequent visiting professor at the University of Hawaii, worked with Norm on a management audit of the Hawaii Department of Corrections. Their 1989 report to the governor and the legislature documented problems in the jails and correctional institutions in Hawaii, and they suggested a number of steps to improve jail and prison administration in that state. This report provided "the broad outline of how a correctional system should operate in order to provide a framework for our recommendations."[10]

Typical of most evaluations of this nature, few of their recommendations were adopted. The recommendations were sound, everyone agreed, but leadership was lacking and resources were not made available to implement change in a correctional system badly in need of reform. Yet, what was significant about this consulting was that its report presented an outline of the proper way to organize and manage a department of corrections, including the development of goals and objectives for the department, the promotion and training of institutional staff, the provision of organizational structure and operation, and a discussion of the programs necessary in a humane correctional system.[11]

Since his retirement in 1987, Norm has also been involved in evaluations of the Department of Corrections in Utah, Michigan, and Illinois in which he had a little more success in getting his recommendations incorporated into penal policy of these states. Norm was also involved in several court cases. He served as special master for the U.S. District Court in Maryland, from 1998-2003, in connection with a class action case involving conditions at the former Baltimore County Jail, *Duvall v. Schaefer*.[12] Baltimore was known to have one of the worst jails in the nation, one badly in need of reform.

From 1997-2002, he served as special monitor for the U.S. District Court, Southern District of New York in the *Sheppard v. Phoenix* case. During 1996, he served as a court appointed expert for the U.S. District Court in Maryland, in connection with a case involving the Maryland Department of Corrections. The ensuing court orders brought considerable improvements to these correctional systems.

Board Participation

Following his retirement as Director of the Bureau of Prisons, Norm continued his involvement on the Advisory Board of the National Institute of Corrections. With his long commitment to staff training and development, he wanted to maintain his support of the provision of training for both local and state correctional agencies, as well as other programs. He also has been on the Board of Directors for the St. Paul's Police foundation for the past ten years.

In the 1990s, he became a member of the board of directors of The GEO Corporation. John Hurley, a former warden with the Bureau of Prisons and current vice president of correctional operations of GEO, has this to say about Norm's participation on the Board:

> Norm has served as an extremely valuable and important member of the Board of Directors. His wisdom and insight into "corrections matters" has assisted other Board members in truly understanding the nature of the corrections world and that has provided a comfort on what to get excited about and what not to. There's no way I can thank Norm for his constant support and guidance. His presence on the Board helps me tremendously.

Scholarly Activities

Norm has also participated in management studies of the U.S. Immigration and Naturalization Service and the Bureau of Indian Affairs. In 1999, Norm, Karen Hess, and Christine Orthman authored *Corrections in the 21st Century*. Wadsworth/Thompson published this textbook for undergraduate corrections students.

Spokesperson for Corrections

Norm continues to be present in corrections functions. He and his wife attend annual Congresses of Correction of the American Correctional Association as well as their winter meetings. He participates in functions of the Bureau of Prisons, including retirement get-togethers.

Conclusions

Since retirement, Carlson has lost his first wife, parents, and sister. Yet, he has celebrated the successes of his two children, has been a proud grandfather, and has happily remarried. After he retired from the Bureau of Prisons, he has continued to influence the field of corrections as a board member, educator, and consultant.

Endnotes

1. Steve Grzegorek was interviewed August 2005.

2. Steve Schwalb was interviewed November 2005.

3. David Ward, Ph.D., was interviewed October 2005.

4. Ibid.

5. Ibid.

6. Incident reported to author by David Ward, Ph.D. (winter of 2008).

7. David Ward, Ph.D., was interviewed October 2007.

8. Ibid.

9. *Sheppard et al. v. Phoenix et al.*, 91 Civil 4148, U.S. District Court, Southern District of New York, 1999.

10. David Ward, Ph.D. and Norm Carlson. 1989. *Management Audit of the Department of Corrections of the State of Hawaii*. February. Report to the Governor and the Legislature of the State of Hawaii, p. 45.

11. Ibid.

12. Civil Action No. k-76-1255 1988.

13. John Hurley sent this e-mail in November 2005.

Part II — Outstanding Leadership and Paradigm Shifts

Chapter 7

Personal Attributes and Outstanding Leadership

[Stonewall] Jackson was not only a judge of character but he could place men in a position to which they were best suited... Old Jack had asked them to do their best, and that was enough to command their most strenuous efforts. ...

His creed may not be ours; but in whom shall we find a firmer fact, a mind more humble, a sincerity more absolute? He had his temptations like the rest of us. His passions were strong; his temper was hot; forgiveness never came easily to him, and he loved power. ...

He saw into the heart of things, both human and divine, far deeper than most men. He had an extraordinary facility for grasping the essential and discarding the extraneous. His language was simple and direct, without elegance or embellishment, and yet no one has excelled him in crystallizing great principles in a single phrase. The few maxims which fell from his lips are almost a complete summary of the art of war.

Colonel G. F. Henderson[1]

Stonewall Jackson was an outstanding general of the Confederate army during the Civil War. Jackson had a number of attributes that marked him for leadership. They came from the influence of family life, his character, and his faith in God. He was a Presbyterian and had a strong belief that God had called him to an important service. He was a man of action; he rose early and liked early risers; and he had amazing powers of deduction. When given an order, his vivid imagination and quick intelligence would determine how he could most effectively execute it.[2]

Norman A. Carlson also has a number of similar personal attributes that contributed to the outstanding leadership he demonstrated as Director of the Bureau of Prisons. These attributes, in turn, enabled the Bureau to become an even more outstanding agency, particularly in the seventeen years he was director. Some of these attributes were due to the influences of his family life; others he developed on the job during the thirty years he worked for the Bureau. "Greatness" was one of the words interviewees frequently used to describe his leadership.

Interviewees were reluctant to find fault with him or to suggest that any personal attributes negatively affected the quality of his leadership. Even when given an opportunity to reflect on Carlson's impatience, which he freely acknowledges as one of his shortcomings, respondents would agree, chuckle, and some would proceed by relating an anecdote demonstrating his impatience.

Significantly, interviewees articulated a strong consensus about Norm's most dominant attributes. The majority listed humility, command presence, integrity, and pursuit of excellence. The perceptions of respondents were remarkably similar, regardless if they worked with the director early or late in his career.

Those interviewed included people in the Bureau of Prisons who Norm picked and promoted, and outside the Bureau—from the Attorney General's office, to members of Congress, and to academics who had contact with Carlson. All were impressed with his leadership. Not surprisingly, eighty interviewees gave glowing statements. Perhaps there are some who were passed over, who felt they were unfairly disciplined, who thought they were on the director's "down" list, who never got over their fear of him, or who did not share his philosophy and vision of the Bureau, and no doubt they would have different things to say.

Our overall interpretation of a person affects how we evaluate his or her personal attributes. If we are positive about someone's leadership, we tend to evaluate their detracting attributes far differently, than if we feel negatively about their leadership. The former brings a forgiving response, while the latter generates a much more critical or judgmental response. Without question, interviewees' fondness for Norm Carlson's leadership made them respond to his positive and detracting traits differently than if they were negative about his leadership.

Command Presence

Norman A. Carlson's tall frame and short crew cut quickly identified him in any group. Yet, his command presence went beyond his physical size, as the following comments illustrate. Gil Ingram, who worked directly with Norm during most of the time he was Director of the Bureau, said "Norm has a 'command presence' before the term was overused. Whether dealing with members of Congress, Attorneys General, fellow correctional leaders, his own staff or inmates, Norm's presence in his room was noted and valued."[3] John Hurley, a former warden, added, "Norm had the ability to always demonstrate that he was in command. His 'rock solid' presence inspired others to perform at the highest levels. Nobody wanted to let Norm down so they worked extra hard to make sure that they were following Norm's directives and expectations."[4]

Pat Keohane, a former warden and regional director, explained: "Norm was a real physical presence. This was exhibited by the way he carried himself, his military bearing, his short hair, his posture, his mannerisms, the way he would issue orders, and the respect he had from the staff and the inmates."[5] Margaret Hambrick, another former warden, provided a visual view, "Norm was so big, physically as well as in personality, that he dominated everything and everyone."[6] Another interviewee quoted an inmate who probably had his command presence in mind when he said about Carlson, "He looks like the Bureau of Prisons."[7]

Humility

Norm Carlson's sense of humility was one of the attributes most frequently cited by interviewees. They commonly related Norm's humility to his greatness. Mary Rawlings, his personal secretary for fifteen of the seventeen years he was director, noted: "His ego never got in the way. One of the things I think is most important about him is he remained humble. He still carpooled even though he bought a second car. I was always impressed by that."[8] Bill Story, another who worked closely with Norm through his career, perhaps summarized it the best: "Norm is not one to blow his own horn. He is very ego-neutral. I have never seen a leader like him who has no concern with padding his own ego."[9]

Carlson's humility affected him in several ways. Roy Gerard, who like several others in the Bureau began their careers in Iowa with Carlson, suggested:

> He is very modest—a quality not often found in a leader, but always found in a good leader. He would always give credit to staff when credit was due. He shared our successes with all staff, particularly the line staff. He emphasized that every position was important and that our accomplishments were a group effort."[10]

Rawlings, his secretary, noted, "He always had me rent a small car, not a large car. Later on, he went up to a medium-sized car. This was the same with hotel accommodations. Unless a conference was at a certain hotel, he would have me rent a Budget Eight. He wouldn't even stay in a Holiday Inn."[11] When he became director, he ordered removal of Director Bennett's very large, unique desk. Some staff members thought that he asked for its removal because it was too big and too showy for him.

The late Pat Sledge, his personal assistant, said, "When Norm retired, we had the same furnishings that we had when I first got there several years before. He did not allow the Director's office any extravagance or semblance of elitism."[12] Thus, Norman A. Carlson's humility resulted in his living very simply, in giving others credit for what was taking place in the Bureau rather than assuming it himself, and in Sherman Day's words never "flaunting the power he had. His power came from his integrity. I can't remember one instance where he ever abused his great reputation or power he had."[13]

Pursuit of Excellence

The pursuit of excellence has always been a major theme of his career. In the Director's Letter of August 18, 1983, sent to assistant directors, regional directors, and wardens, Norm Carlson wrote, "On many occasions, I have talked about the need to set high standards and demand excellence. I recently came across the following quote in the book, *The Search of Excellence*, by Thomas J. Peters and Robert H. Waterman, Jr.:

> Set and demand standards of excellence. Anyone who accepts mediocrity—in school, in joy, in life—is a guy who compromises. And when the leader compromises, the whole damn organization compromises.[14]

Carlson's high expectations created considerable anxiety in the field, especially when the Director was coming for a visit. Gil Ingram said, "He didn't condone mediocrity."[15] Sam Samples, one of the pivotal figures in the staff-training movement of the Bureau, added, "His expectations were extremely high for every single employee, especially for management employees. He not only expected excellence, but he demanded it. There simply was no room for error, poor judgment, or inefficiency."[16] No one wanted to let Norm down. Ingram related an incident which expressed how intense staff were to fulfill what the director desired:

The situation involved a helicopter escape from the Western Region. Norm was aware of it in detail before the chief correctional officer in Central Office (who was responsible for operational security policy in this area) was aware. This supervisor made a mistake in using the restroom next to the Director's office. He found himself in the Director's presence, learned of the escape there in the restroom, received instructions on how to follow up, heard about the Director's feeling concerning the matter, and ruined a new pair of shoes in approximately three minutes. He followed up very nicely with the matter but never again used that restroom. He clearly became so engrossed with listening to this man who he deeply respected (and momentarily feared) that he forgot where he was and what he was doing.[17]

Integrity

Integrity was the personal attribute that most respondents noted. Patrick Keohane, a former warden, echoed the responses of many when he said "He was… squeaky clean."[18] He amplified this when he described Norm's response following the 1983 murders of two officers at the U.S. Penitentiary, Marion, Illinois: "Norm told us to get control there and make sure no one [inmates] got abused. He wanted it professionally done. We knew there were boundaries and not to cross over into anything that was illegal, unethical, or immoral."[19]

Roy Gerard added, "Norm was and is a model of "clean living. He would not tolerate any bad apples in the Bureau. He was not only a great leader; he was a good husband, father, and friend. These attributes carried over in his everyday work and were demonstrated often enough so that his integrity was not questioned."[20] Robert Levinson, Ph.D., the father of unit management, highlighted the issue of Norm's integrity in an even sharper way:

> Norm was the embodiment of integrity. Anything that even had the vaguest hint of a conflict of interest was avoided. This applied not only to his own dealings with the myriad of

issues he had to cope with, but it also applied to staff at all levels—in both the Central Office and the field facilities. It was also well known that any improprieties on the part of staff toward inmates (or other staff) were given high priority by him and received immediate attention. Resolution was swift and 'punishment" meted out accordingly.[21]

Personal Grounding

Norman A. Carlson's values and strong support system from his earliest years at home seemed to anchor him. It was a widespread contention that with his Iowa upbringing and his Midwestern background, he was solid and others could count on him. Sherman Day, Ph.D., put it this way: "He was grounded in what he wanted to do, a person of great integrity and openness. Consequently, in a time of turmoil, he was the anchor for corrections in America."[22] Staff felt that his "groundedness" enabled him to be "cool" under pressure. He could handle all the difficult problems, including contacts with politicians on the Hill; and he would always be under control. Several staff members said that they had never heard Norm raise his voice or swear.

Gary Mote, the architect who helped shape the prison construction of the Bureau in the 1970s, perhaps best captured Norm's "groundedness" in the following statement:

> Norm is a person of high moral character. While I know only a little of Norm's formative early life, I think it is safe to assume that he grew up in a family with strong values and principles, including strong religious values. . . . I mention it only to emphasize that it was apparent to me that he lived his religious beliefs every day. Not on his sleeve; he never spoke to me, or any of the staff that I was aware of, about his religious convictions, but they were evident by his actions and example. In my view, this is perhaps the best way to exercise one's faith in most daily activity. The only overt religious "signal" I recall was, on a few occasions, to suggest a

moment of silence during a meeting. I don't remember a specific instance, but the death of an officer or other staff would have been a likely reason. I also knew he and his family attended Lutheran church services regularly.[23]

Mote went on to describe how his first wife, Pat, was a strong and stabilizing influence on his career and life. "Pat," he said, "was a fine person; a very good wife and mother. She had equally high values, also based largely on her faith, I think. She was energetic, eminently sensible, very supportive and seemed to have excellent judgment in matters of both people and issues." Mote continued, "She never said so out loud, around me at any rate, but my guess is that she helped him sort through many issues of the day."[24]

Order and Cleanliness

As Bob Levinson put it, "Norm was fastidious." He continued, "Everything—in both the Central Office and the Bureau's facilities—was maintained in a spotless, polished, orderly fashion. While there were some behind-the-hands smiles about this, nevertheless his approach set a very positive tone."[25] Margaret Hambrick, former Bureau warden, added:

> I clearly remember Norm's visits. All institutions had to be scrupulously clean! We kept them that way. It was a hallmark of how we ran a prison. However, when Norm was coming, we tried to take it to the next level. Of particular concern was the first bathroom next to the front door. Norm always had to go when he first came in the door. That restroom got extra attention.[26]

Norm was aware that his culture of order and cleanliness was symbolic of an important truth: that a clean institution reveals that the staff are in charge. Conversely, a dirty prison demonstrates that inmates are in charge and the consequence will ultimately be violence and disorder.

Acuity of Mind

Those who spent time around Norm usually remarked on his intelligence. Gary Mote commented: "He is unusually quick of mind. He plods through correspondence, briefing papers and reports speedily, while taking phone calls if need be, sorts out the issues, and retains both the essence and the details."[27] In Exhibit 7.1, Rick Seiter, Ph.D., a former warden, examines the relationship between Norm Carlson's keen intelligence, analytical skills, visionary status, and the fact that he became a legendary figure:

Exhibit 7.1 A True Visionary

"First of all, what made him so legendary is that he is a true visionary. I think what makes him such a visionary is his ability to analyze. He has a very analytical mind, as well as being innovative and visionary. He is more analytical than he is visionary, and he uses that to build his vision. He looks at where we have been, what the issues are, and he is really adept about picking up little tidbits, about what is going on in corrections and in the Bureau of Prisons or what he picks up from political leaders or elected officials.

"He is able to say, 'I see the path and the direction that we need to go. With the opportunity I have to hear from a variety of people, it is possible to put these kinds of pieces in perspective.' He could envision where corrections was going to be three years from now, five years from now, and ten years from now. Then, his real strength was that he was so proactive he would move the Bureau of Prisons there before anybody else could get there, before it became an in-thing to do, and before politicians began to push in a certain way. He would get there before there was any emergency to get you there or before there was any political expediency. He was always seen as leading the way in a visionary way, but I don't think it was visionary as much as he was a great listener and one who could see where the forces were going to push us and to be ahead of the game."

Source: Interviewed December 2005.

Norm was also able to see in ways that others did not see. Patrick Keohane expressed this well when he said that Norm could walk through an institution and "see things that people who had been there for fifteen-to-twenty years had not seen. He could spot a good thing or a bad thing."[28] Bill Story added, "People have said how intuitive he was. He could see things that other people couldn't see."[29] When asked, how did he do this? Story answered, "He just seemed to have the innate ability to quickly perceive what was going on in an institution, and I can't tell you why. He just did."[30]

Michael Quinlan, who followed Norm as director of the Bureau of Prisons, observed that Norm was also a good synthesizer. "He has an ability to synthesize things better than most people. He is able to take information, see the value, [know] what the right direction is, and articulate this in a very clear, concise, and direct way." Quinlan continued, "So that everybody, regardless whether he was meeting with two or three people or in a room of fifty, you get it. You see it; it is clear. He has done this so many hundreds of times, and it never ceases to amaze me."[31]

Avid Reader

Norm has been a prolific reader all his life. Throughout his career, Norm read the *New York Times*, the *Washington Post*, and the *Wall Street Journal* every day. He was always looking for some book or publication for profitable reading. Gary Mote added, "He kept himself 'well read' and informed on the major social, organizational, and political issues of the day."[32] Quinlan added, "I always felt that he really knows how to concentrate. When I would see Norm, as his executive assistant, and he wasn't involved in an issue, or a meeting, or working on correspondence, he would be reading. There were always books that would help him grow. He never stopped learning."[33]

Quinlan captured what gave impetus to Norm's desire to read and that was his commitment to a growth model. He believed that life is a process of becoming, and as part of this process, we continue to learn. One way to do this is to read and to expose yourself to the ideas of others or surrounded yourself by individuals who expose you to new ideas. Another way is to learn from your mistakes. Norm excelled in all three of these.

"Stormin' Norman"

Early in his career in the field he became known as "Stormin' Norman." Charlie Turnbo, a former Bureau of Prisons staff member who was in charge of training, thought he was called "Stormin' Norman" because "he was an assertive director, quick walking, quick talking, quick paced, and a Northerner."[34] Eugene Barkin contributed that "in the field he was Stormin' Norman. When he came in, he came in like a bull in a china shop."[35]

John Hurley, a former Bureau of Prisons warden, added his version of why Norm was given this name. "When Norm got upset, you did-not want to be around. He became a man on a mission, and he would 'storm' wherever he wanted to or needed to get people's attention and get the answers or response he wanted. Remember, he was a big man, and I think sometimes it scared the hell out of people."[36] Wade Houk, an assistant director of the Bureau, remarked, "When Norm was angry, you could instantly sense it. It would be through the air."[37]

Bill Story, another Bureau of Prisons staff member, explained: "I think his physical stature had a little bit to do with it. When he came into an institution, he was ready to go. He was ready to see what was happening and to communicate with both staff and inmates. He was not interested in a partial tour; he wanted to go throughout the institution and to inspect every area."[38]

Those who worked in correctional institutions often feared the "Big Swede," a taskmaster who expected them to meet his high expectations. Many did not look forward to his visiting the institution, especially if he had found problems before in their prison. They concurred that Norm had no problem informing individuals that they had fallen down on their duties. He would say it quietly but firmly, "You did not do what you should have done."

Kind, Gentle, and Gracious Person

Interestingly, those who knew Norm well, especially those who had worked with him in the Central Office or had been around for any length of time, almost always perceived him as a very kind, gentle, and gracious person.

Pat Sledge, his personal assistant, put this very well:

> Norm was a sweet teddy bear to work for. While some people saw him so much differently, those around him every day knew what he really was. Norm had heartfelt empathy and concern for staff who were hurting. He showed this to us in our office and with our families. . . . While he could not go out and be with people all over the Bureau, if he learned about someone who suffered a loss or should be congratulated, he would call in his secretary, and dictate his own letter to them. He did not have to do this, but he did.[39]

Jim Meko, a former warden, noted, "Norm would mix with everyone." He added, "Norm always had time for the GS-4 guy who worked in the mailroom and delivered mail to his office. As the person who had worked in the mailroom for a long time told me one day, 'Norm Carlson reminded him of another man. The only politician he ever saw in operation was Bobby Kennedy who came through the building and shook hands with everyone.' That is the way Norm Carlson operates too."[40]

Russell Gaines, Norm's former driver, added, "He treated me and everyone else in the office fairly. He treated everybody the same and that is the right way. He was impartial. I have never seen him treat anybody unfairly. He is a good man."[41] Michelle Humphrey, Norm's personal secretary the final two years he was director, said: "I think that people were intimidated by him. If you got to know the real Norm, he was just as nice as he could be." She went on, "Norm liked ice cream. He would send out and buy everyone ice cream. He would bring us fresh vegetables."[42]

Pat Samples, who worked on training issues, commented, "He was also very gracious in so many ways. He is a kind man, has a good heart, and is a very moral person." He added a personal note, "I remember that my wife's mother died in 1981. When we got back home from the funeral, there was a letter to my wife from Norm expressing sympathy for her mother's death. That made a forever-lasting impression on her, and she appreciated that so much. He was good at doing that kind of stuff."[43]

In Exhibit 7.2, Bob Matthews, a former Bureau of Prisons warden and regional director, contributed another view of what a good human being Norm Carlson is.

Exhibit 7.2 Norm is a Warm and Kind Human Being

"When I was selected as U.S. Marshal for the District of Columbia, I lived in D.C. by myself for six months while my wife was teaching junior college in Ashland, Kentucky. Norm and Pat would invite me over for dinner most Sundays. He is just that kind of person. When my wife came, we would get together at Christmas and other times. I got to know him socially as well as professionally.

"There was a side of Norm that people saw that was tough and 'no-nonsense.' But there was another side to him that not so many people saw. He was a guy with a warm heart, and a genuine good human being. I got a chance to see that side of him. Norm had a great sense of humor; he would laugh when you spun a good yarn. He laughed at others' jokes. It took a certain toughness to run the agency, but, on the other hand, Norm is as warm and kind a human being as you would ever want to find."

Source: Interviewed October 2005.

Cool Under Fire

One of Norm Carlson's most impressive personal attributes was his ability to be "cool under fire," according to two former Assistant Directors of the Bureau of Prisons, Gary Mote and Gil Ingram. Gary Mote expressed it simply, "He did not let his emotions get in the way of the issues and solutions."[44] Gil Ingram added, "Norm remained patient and steadfast in times of stress and emergency. His resoluteness and calm demeanor reassured those around him." Steve Schwalb, warden and former head of the Internal Affairs Unit, further noted, "During tough times, during some difficult budget times, and during times like when he had to designate John Mitchell to prison on Watergate, he always seemed to be completely at ease, down-home, common, and a decent person."[45]

Bureau staff related a number of incidents of Norm behaving coolly under fire. When there were nine murders over seven months at Lewisburg, he transferred out the warden, two associate wardens, and a captain and implemented unit management. Subsequently, only one murder occurred in the next eighteen months.[46] What was so significant was that Norm told a Bureau staff member he felt if there had been another murder right away, the Attorney General would have changed directors of the Bureau.[47]

Remarkable Memory

Norm's ability to recall names was a personal trait that nearly every former staff member identified. Gary Mote put it this way: "Another invaluable trait is his uncanny ability to remember names. I was with him in many different settings, including our travels, when he would greet by name someone he had not seen in a very long time, and might not have known too well. I was never around anyone who exceeded his ability in this regard."[48] Former Bureau of Prisons Director Mike Quinlan added, "He has a fabulous memory. I am amazed how even today Norm would see people that he knew in the Bureau, and not necessarily senior people, and Norm would remember their names."[49]

Without depreciating in any way Norm's outstanding memory, Loy Hayes, Jr., Bureau staffer, noted that he had a system that helped him in this process. Loy said, "He knew so many people, but he would always keep someone near him who knew who the local people were. Although he was very good at calling people by their names, he was also smart at having people near him who knew who they were. The people near him could refresh his memory about the staff that they would be bumping into. He actually remembered inmates' names, too."[50]

Good Physical Health

Norm Carlson always had good health during the thirty years he worked for the Bureau of Prisons. Mary Rawlings, Norman Carlson's personal secretary for fifteen years, said Norm did not have health problems, "Not that he complained of. He was at work all the time."[51] Still, Carlson, as many of us, suffered with allergy problems throughout his career. Dr. Robert Brutsche, former medical director of the Bureau, noted,

> Norm had allergies and took shots for this. The nurse used to give them to him. He also had me give them to him, especially if we were on a trip. One time on a trip, we didn't have any alcohol, so I just put some gin on his arm. He said, 'this smells like gin.' I said, 'Yes, it is rubbing alcohol.'" He just laughed and laughed."[52]

Charles Turnbo, a former Bureau of Prisons warden, tells of a serious allergic reaction.

> I remember one incident. We were at an FBI meeting, he ate something that had nuts in it, and he had quite a reaction. I knew I had to get him to the hospital because I was afraid we were going to lose him. When I got him to the car, I discovered that I had locked the keys in the car. I was frantically trying to find someone, FBI agent or anyone, to help me get

the car unlocked. We finally got him to the hospital, and he was given something for the allergy reaction and was all right.[53]

Impatience

When I asked Norm what was his greatest flaw, he said, "Impatience."[54] Indeed, at former staff get-togethers, Norm's impatience was frequently one of the legendary stories that they told. A former staff member tells of the time that the executive staff was in California, and they were going to the prison at Pleasanton. "The prison van was supposed to pick us up at 6:00 a.m. I got down there at ten of six, and the van was gone. Norm got there and was ready to go. He couldn't stand to wait."[55]

Several others noted that Norm could not stand to waste time. One former staff member explained, "He couldn't stand to wait longer than five minutes in an airport lounge. He would leave his office for a 2:00 p.m. flight at 1:30 p.m., and the driver would deliver him at National Airport at ten of two. He would walk to the gate in five minutes and then be five minutes ahead of time. I checked with his secretary, and he only missed one plane a year."[56]

Conclusions

The quality of a person's leadership cannot be divorced from the attributes that he or she brings to the job. If the overall effect of what a person brings to the table is positive, then we forgive those detracting characteristics or traits. Norm's thirty-years of leadership in the Bureau of Prisons, especially the seventeen years he was Director, were those in which his humility, integrity, desire for excellence, mental acuity, and coolness under fire contributed to his outstanding leadership. These personal characteristics earned him such credibility and respect among most Bureau staff that they overlooked other less desirable qualities, such as his impatience.

One of the dominant characteristics of Norman A. Carlson's leadership is that he is able to perform effectively in many areas. Due to his ability to attain this high performance in different aspects of management, people frequently used the terms "outstanding" and "excellent" to describe his leadership. Nearly all agreed that they could not separate the high quality of the director's performance from the personal attributes that he brought to his job.

Endnotes

1. Colonel G. F. R. Henderson, *Stonewall Jackson and the American Civil War.* New York: Barnes and Noble, pp. 434, 712, and 713.

2. Ibid.

3. Gil Ingram sent an e-mail August 2005.

4. John Hurley was interviewed September 2005.

5. Pat Keohane was interviewed September 2005.

6. Margaret Hambrick was interviewed November 2005.

7. Pat Keohane was interviewed October 2005.

8. Mary Rawlings was interviewed August 2005.

9. Bill Story was interviewed August 2005.

10. Roy Gerard sent these comments in an e-mail August 2005.

11. Mary Rawlings was interviewed August 2005.

12. Pat Sledge was interviewed August 2005.

13. Sherman Day, Ph.D., was interviewed August 2005.

14. Letter from the Director on August 18, 1983.

15. Gil Ingram sent an e-mail August 2005.

16. Sam Staples, Ph.D., was interviewed September 2005.

17. Gil Ingram sent an e-mail August 2005.

18 Pat Keohane was interviewed October 2005.

19. Ibid.

20. Gil Ingram sent an e-mail August 2005.

21. Robert Levinson, Ph.D., sent an e-mail August 2005.

22. Sherman Day, Ph.D., was interviewed August 2005.

23. Gary Mote was interviewed October 2005.

24. Ibid.

25. Robert Levinson, Ph.D., sent an e-mail August 2005.

26. Margaret Hambrick was interviewed November 2005.

27. Gary Mote was interviewed October 2005.

28. Pat Keohane was interviewed October 2005.

29. Bill Story was interviewed September 2005.

30. Ibid.

31. Michael Quinlan was interviewed November 2005.

32. Gary Mote was interviewed October 2005.

33. Michael Quinlan was interviewed November 2005.

34. Charles Turnbo was interviewed September 2005

35. Eugene Baskin was interviewed August 2005.

36. John Hurley sent this e-mail November 2005.

37. Bill Story was interviewed August 2005.

38. Wade Houk was interviewed August 2005.

39. Pat Sledge was interviewed August 2005.

40. Jim Meko was interviewed August 2005.

41. Russell Gaines was interviewed August 2005.

42. Michelle Humphrey was interviewed August 2005.

43. Pat Samples was interviewed October 2005.

44. Gary Mote was interviewed December 2005.

45. Gil Ingram sent this e-mail August 2005.

46. Steve Schwalb was interviewed December 2005.

47. Steve Grzegorek was interviewed August 2005.

48. Gary Mote was interviewed October 2005.

49. Michael Quinlan was interviewed December 2005.

50. Loy Hayes, Jr. was interviewed August 2005.

51. Mary Rawlings was interviewed October 2005.

52. Dr. Robert Brutsche was interviewed October 2005.

53. Charles Turnbo was interviewed September 2005.

54. Norm Carlson was interviewed 2005.

55. Anonymous staff member was interviewed August 2005.

56. Anonymous staff member was interviewed August 2005.

Chapter 8

Management and Principles of Leadership

The interesting thing is that even though I did not work directly with Mr. Carlson, I felt like I knew him from almost the first year of my employment. I think anyone who worked for the Bureau would during his tenure say the same thing. Norm just had this ability to always be in command and everyone had this comfort that everything would be all right as long as "Norm was running things." His presence was always there. Whether through policy guidelines, new programs and initiatives, personal visits to the facilities, newsletters, or just "folklore" passed on from warden to warden, he was the boss and everyone knew it.

John Hurley, former Bureau of Prisons Warden[1]

Norm was first and foremost so grounded in sound corrections management principles. The Bureau of Prisons was looked at as a model by state systems. It was the measuring stick by which a state system would always say—this is what the Bureau is doing, and this is what we are doing. I always believed that this is what Norm intended the Bureau to be under his tenure.

Steve J. Martin, corrections consultant

This chapter focuses on the quality of Norm Carlson's leadership while he was Director of the Federal Bureau of Prisons. To evaluate his management skills, we will examine four aspects of his leadership: (1) the principles of management that he believed in, (2) his management style and how he used this style, (3) the quality of life that he developed in the Bureau of Prisons, and (4) how he handled situations that arose during the seventeen years he led the agency. One of the most impressive aspects of his leadership is that interviewees perceived how he was leading the agency in such similar ways. In spite of the numbers of individuals who were interviewed, some of whom had much more direct contact with Carlson than others, the responses were remarkably alike.

One of the limitations of this study is that it was not a random selected sample. It is composed of those who agreed to be interviewed. Again, as stated in the last chapter, if it were possible to interview those who had not been promoted, who felt that they had been treated unfairly, or who were totally intimidated by the director, they might take this opportunity to express their unhappiness, especially toward Director Carlson. In other words, any disgruntlement would probably be reflected in this chapter; their view of Carlson's management principles and how he ran the Bureau would be much different than what is here.

Some did fault Carlson's philosophy. A number of Bureau staff did not share his management philosophy; some felt that he was too liberal and gave inmates far too many rights and privileges; others felt that he was too conservative in his interpretation of how a prison should be run. Some Bureau staff did not feel the director was doing enough to protect them from inmates. The hiring of ex-offenders came under some criticism, and some staff questioned whether color TVs in dayrooms was coddling inmates.

On Capitol Hill, Norm Carlson met the same reaction. Some senators and members of Congress felt that he was too liberal; others felt that he was too conservative. Alvin J. Bronstein, former Director of the American Civil Liberties Union Prison Project, questioned how the Bureau and Carlson handled several cases during Carlson's administration. Both inside and outside of Congress, some charged that "country club prisons" were unnecessary. They also questioned whether the progressive institutional designs were a waste of taxpayers' money. Furthermore, some said that the Watergate offenders and other white-collar inmates received special treatment. For example, some questioned John Mitchell having surgery outside the prison setting.

The fact still remains that the negative reaction of a few does not negate Norman Carlson's significant contributions to the Federal Bureau of Prisons. And even on a more global perspective, no administrator in corrections or any other bureaucracy can satisfy everyone. There are always those who have their grievances, some of them legitimate, against the organization for which they work. The embittered, or the disillusioned, few, however, do not erase the larger good that an effective organization is accomplishing.

Principles of Management

Norman A. Carlson employed several management principles that did not vary a great deal from the time he became director in 1970 to the day he retired in 1987.

- He believed in leading by example. He emphasized to the staff the following points:
    - Everyone from the director to the line officer was a public servant.
    - Everyone worked for the public.
    - Image was extremely important. He cut no corners in his own behavior. He avoided controversies by not allowing personal privileges for staff, such as first-class accommodations, conferences at resort cities, or luxury cars.[2]
- He believed in pursuing excellence in whatever he did, and he wanted his staff to adopt this attitude as well.
- He had a fundamental respect for the law, and this affected his managerial decisions on all levels.

- He believed in a hands-on approach to prison administration, which is sometimes referred to as the "management by walking around" (MBWA) approach to running a prison. In his institutional tours, it was not unusual for him to ask an inmate what the warden looked like. The institutional warden, of course, was a step behind the rapidly walking director. If the inmate did not know the warden, then the warden was in a heap of trouble.
- He believed in a clean institution because excellence began when the prison was clean and orderly. Staff felt good about it, and even some inmates felt good about it. A variety of stories existed about what wardens did to make their institutions shine when the director was coming.
- He rewarded good performance but did not condone mediocrity.[3]
- Norm was proactive before the term became popular. He believed it was important to get ahead of the curve. He saw emerging trends and issues that should be addressed early. He did not believe in permitting problems to simmer any longer than necessary. Yet, he was good at distinguishing ephemeral issues and not acting precipitously.[4]
- Norm believed it was important to align responsibilities with individual talents. If individuals were not working out at a particular position, Norm attempted to find a position better suited to their talents. He would put them in a less visible, less stressful, and less demanding position.[5]
- He communicated to staff exactly what he desired. He wanted staff to know where he was going and what he expected. However, once he let you know what he wanted, then he got out of your way and let you do it.[6]
- He went a long way with staff as long as they were honest, had integrity, and were trying hard, but if they behaved with a lack of integrity, they knew that their behavior was not going to be tolerated.[7]
- He believed that it was important to listen to people—to be sensitive to what they were saying and to be objective before making up his mind.[8]

- He showed a commitment to mentoring and helping staff achieve their fullest potential.
- He believed he and his staff must not only be right, but they must look right because perception is reality. He showed them that you have to be aware of and realize how people perceive what you are doing.[9]
- His position was that where you stand on a subject depends on where you sit. Or to express this in another way, the position you occupy or hold influences the position you take.[10]
- He strongly believed that you treat all people—citizens, staff, and inmates with respect— without regard to race, ethnicity, creed, sexual orientation, or political position.[11]
- He held that all staff members are part of the Bureau family.[12]
- He believed that you needed to keep up with what was going on in the world. You should not isolate yourself. He kept informed of current events through newspapers, CNN, and network news.[13]
- His applied a balanced approach to management. Public safety was always paramount, but ensuring the rights of inmates, giving inmates opportunities to change and improve themselves, and reducing recidivism were also important purposes of corrections.[14]
- He wanted to hear the viewpoints of those he considered the most knowledgeable on particular issues. So, he was continuously receptive to what Norval Morris, John Dilulio, James Jacobs, James Q. Wilson, Walter Menninger, and other thinkers had to contribute.
- He was always on the lookout for talent. One former warden described an incident when Norm came back from his walking tour of the institution and questioned, "What do you think about Mary Brown, the case worker from Cellblock B?" He responded, 'Norm, she is top notch. She is a great employee. She is going to be up there and be considered for warden one of these days.' He never forgot talent. We all know that he has a tremendous memory for names and faces and may have

forgotten about Mary Brown; yet, a year and a half later when somebody was looking for a particular person, he remembered her. So, he would promote her."[15]
- He saw the big picture, but, at the same time, was concerned about detail. The ability to perceive the big picture was why staff often saw him as visionary, but the concern for detail was how he was able to attain excellence.

What was remarkable about the management of Norman Carlson was that Bureau staff were aware of his principles. They bought into the importance of these principles, and they worked hard to realize these principles in the management and operations of their institutions. In a real sense, then, the principles of the director became the principles of his loyal staff, which largely contributed to why Norm Carlson was able to attain the level of excellence that he desired.

Style of Leadership

Norm Carlson's appointment as director in 1970, as previously suggested, posed several problems for him: (1) He had no time to prepare or anticipate what he would do, because of the complete surprise to others and at least some surprise to himself; (2) he was known as a treatment person and treatment staff were not given much credibility among custodial staff; and (3) he had no experience as a warden or associate warden, ordinarily considered mandatory to advancement up the ladder of the Bureau of Prisons; and (4) he was young—thirty-six years of age.

He quickly came to the conclusion that his style of management must be such that it would include the following outcomes:

- He became one of the early proactive corrections leaders. He wanted to be anticipatory and preventative, so that institutional problems, as much as possible, could be avoided. His success as a proactive leader was helped by the fact that he was a decision-maker and was skillful in analyzing problems and quickly coming to a decision. Then, he was shrewd enough to find

competent custodial administrators, such as James D. Henderson, who could advise him concerning custodial issues occurring in institutions.
- He placed a high priority on direct communication with both staff and inmates.
- He placed importance on accountability, attention to detail, and timely and firm compliance with schedules and movement. He felt that staff should have control over detail, schedules, and movement in their facility. Unless staff were in control, he knew that inmates would control the prison, with disastrous results.
- He became aware of the importance of selecting, recruiting, and training staff.
- He wanted to make the Federal Bureau of Prisons into a career agency, rather than one in which the intrusion of politics would determine who would be the director of the Bureau of Prisons.
- He wanted the Bureau of Prisons to be a standard-setter for all correctional agencies in their pursuit of excellence.

Shift in Leadership Style

As the years went on, Norman Carlson became more flexible and brought staff more into the decision-making process. Participatory management did not become widely used in corrections until the 1980s, but in the 1970s, Carlson realized that more attention had to be given to a participatory-management style.

This shift in style of leadership was reflected in the executive-staff meetings. At these bimonthly meetings, all assistant and regional directors met at a nearby Bureau facility where they could visit. Topics of the meeting included selection of top-level personnel as well as policy issues. Executive members prepared for these meetings by reviewing prepared papers to help them in assessing, clarifying, and initiating policy.

Steve Grzegorek, a former Bureau of Prisons' Regional Director, talked about the "donnybrooks" that emerged at the executive staff meetings. When questioned whether this meant lively discussion, he said,

> More than that, we almost came to blows some of the time. But the director had the comfort level to let it happen . . . He had enough confidence in himself and his staff that he knew something good would come out of these lively debates . . . and it did. When the day was done, he would say "this is the way we are going." We would end the discussion, and that was our plan. I could be bitterly opposed to the new plan or procedure, but because of his leadership, it was our plan and we were going to carry it out.[16]

During executive meetings with staff, Norm set there listening, fingering his paper clips. He became legendary for the shapes he could twist a paper clip. Those personal traits—impatience, terseness, and a desire not to waste time—made these meetings seem excessive in his mind. Yet, his excellence as a manager made him realize that, beyond his personal desires, these meetings were building collegiality with staff, teaching them to see the larger picture, helping them to make decisions, and making it easier for them to buy into his vision for the Bureau.

As part of his leadership style, Norm Carlson focused on presenting a positive organizational culture in the Bureau based on excellence and integrity-based leadership. Former warden John Hurley described how Norm built a new culture at the Bureau of Prisons:

"Norm was the culture of the Bureau of Prisons. If you were going to work for the Bureau of Prisons you would always
    1. Do your job
    2. Be a professional
    3. Know policy and procedure
    4. Tell the truth, whether it was bad news or good news
    5. Support your leadership
    6. Treat people with dignity (including inmates)

7. Understand that you represented your facility and the agency, both at and away from work
8. Work hard, but enjoy your success and appreciate those around you who contributed to your success.

Norm did that by modeling his behavior, on and off the job, and by every facet of his communication. When you worked for the Bureau of Prisons, you knew you were part of something special and most importantly, that you were contributing to a public service."[17]

The Relationship Between Quality of Life and a Humane Prison

Norm Carlson believed that life in a humane prison should have a number of features. He insisted that all of these features were desirable in the settings provided by the Bureau of Prisons.

Treat Inmates with Decency and Respect. Inmates have a right to be treated with decency and respect. When Frank Wood was warden of the Minnesota Correctional Facilities at Stillwater and Oak Park Heights, he used to say that this meant treating inmates as you would want your father or brother to be treated if he were incarcerated.[18] Norm never put it this way, but this is what he meant.

He believed that it was important to communicate with inmates and let them know that they were persons of value. This is part of the reason that when he would visit an institution, his ritual, which he always followed, was to eat breakfast with the inmates. He would wait in line with them, talking with them, and responding to their concerns. Inmates reacted in a positive way to this Big Swede and felt that the director was concerned about their welfare. Over time, inmates in various prisons got to know Norm, and some even called him "Norm."

Keep Inmates Safe. The safety of inmates must always be a top concern in a humane prison. Many prisoners have a long history of being predators and will continue this behavior in a prison context if given the opportunity. Weaker inmates may find themselves thrust into institutions in which they feel that they are unable to protect themselves. No matter what else takes place, a prison cannot claim to be humane if inmates are being raped, assaulted, and murdered by other inmates. Too many prisoners in the past have done their time in constant dread of being attacked; fear begets fear, and the consequences will always be a more disruptive prison. Some argue that all inmates cannot be protected, because there are so many areas of indefensible space in which the weak can be victimized. The fact is that prison administrators must adopt policy that will more likely ensure the protection of inmates.

Protect Safety of Staff. The rights of staff to be protected also are part of a humane and decent correctional system. Officers know that on any given day they may be assaulted by inmates. Staff assaults are always possible, because regardless of how well a prison is run, incidents are sometimes inevitable. Nevertheless, the warden and associate wardens must make it very clear to inmates that assaults against staff are totally unacceptable and will receive severe consequences. The inmates need to know that the warden's position is very simple: Inmates will be prosecuted by the prison internal disciplinary system, and if they violate any federal or state law, they will be prosecuted by the courts for that and given additional time.

Ensure Some Degree of Privacy. Inmates have the right in a decent correctional system to have some privacy in their cells. They do not have a right to keep contraband in their cells or to engage in illegal acts while in their cells, and for that reason, correctional staff must conduct unannounced cell searches. Privacy also means that inmates' personal property is respected; it needs to be searched but not destroyed. Privacy further includes the respect of restoring the cell to the shape it was in before the search.

Classify Inmates Properly. Carlson believed that proper classification can do much to provide a secure and safe facility. Classification also can be helpful in dealing with troublesome inmates, such as moving them to a different institution or to a more secure unit within that facility. SENTRY, the innovative inmate classification system, was one means the Bureau of Prisons used to classify troublesome inmates and, as a result, to provide for the safety of both inmates and staff. It provided immediate access to the current institutional population or community facility population. SENTRY calculated all aspects of inmates' sentences and is used to assign inmates to specific facilities. SENTRY identifies inmates the court has determined need special evaluation (such as the need to separate inmates who have threatened each other) and records inmates' participation in disruptive groups and street gangs.[19]

Restrict Lockdowns. Locking the facility down for extended periods should be done only on an emergency basis and, when that happens, the staff must take rapid steps to resolve the problems that led to this emergency status. Some inmates cannot be trusted to live peacefully with other inmates. These inmates must be isolated from the rest of the population. For those inmates who do not need extended lockdowns, keeping them locked down for extended periods without good cause is both inhumane policy and crisis-centered management. Doing so is likely to increase problems in the long run.

Control Gang Activities. Carlson held that one group of inmates, such as a prison gang, must not be permitted to control the inmate population. Bureau officials quickly discovered that the only way to operate a prison was to deny the recognition of gangs. They must be given no privileges. This nonrecognition of gangs extended to gang leaders, some of whom may have become legends.

Deflect Racial Tensions. Carlson further recognized that racial tensions must not control prison life and contribute to conflicts and violence. Although there is no simple solution to racial conflict within a prison, what must be communicated is that inmates do not have to like each other, but it is necessary that they get along.

Provide Opportunities for Individual Growth. An important aspect of the quality of life in a humane prison is to provide opportunities for individuals who want to grow and benefit from their confinement. Inmates must have opportunities to learn marketable skills, and be offered educational opportunities and substance-abuse treatment.

Provide Adequate Medical and Dental Services for Inmates. A humane prison must offer adequate medical and dental services. Medical services have become one of the most important and troubling areas because of infectious diseases (such as HIV, AIDS, hepatitis B and C, and tuberculosis), female health issues, mental health problems, and elderly prisoners' medical concerns. The increased lengths of sentences, because of the recently revised criminal codes in most states, have added to the problem. Prisoners are staying longer and more of them are there for the duration of their natural lives. All of this places enormous demands on medical services that have become increasingly costly.

Offer Recreational Services for Inmates. Finally, recreational services are a vital part of the programming of a humane prison. In the 1990s, following the retirement of Norman Carlson, some of the recreational services in prison were heavily criticized by the "make prisoners suffer" or "make prison time hard time" advocates. Recreational services, according to these misled politicians and policymakers, made "doing time" too easy and softened the punishment inmates were supposed to receive in prison.

How Norm Carlson Handled Situations

One of the best ways to ascertain and evaluate a managerial style is to examine how a person handles situations. In the following incidents, Norm Carlson's managerial style becomes apparent.

High-Risk Situation. Steve Grzegorek, former Bureau of Prisons Regional Director, illustrated that Norm could tolerate a lot of pressure. Grzegorek observed how organized-crime inmates were gravitating back to the East Coast. When he looked at his institution, it seemed as if most of the inmates were Italian. He heard that a work stoppage was going to occur. His staff was concerned, but he said, "Let it happen." He felt that it would give him a chance to transfer out the organized crime inmates. "It did happen; there was a work stoppage. Shortly thereafter, I had two buses at the institution, and I had sixty some OC [organized crime] guys taken out and spread out all across the U.S."[20]

When Grzegorek told Norm, he said, "Oh, that's fine! That's good!

That's what we are supposed to do!" However, some repercussions did arise—including a threat on both Grzegorek's and Carlson's lives. There was also a bribe attempt. Carmine "The Snake" Persico bribed one of the correctional officers with $50,000 to get him back to the East Coast. Unknown to him, the FBI was conducting a sting on him. Grzegorek added, "Of course, Norm approved all of those things. He wasn't afraid of 'high risk.'"[21]

AIDS in Prison. Jerry Farkas, former Bureau of Prisons' warden and regional director, described how Norman Carlson was decisive in his decision-making. According to Farkas, when the AIDS issue first came to the fore, no one had a handle on it.

> What Bureau staff knew was that inmates with AIDS were coming into their prisons. They questioned: 'Do you segregate them from the rest of the inmates? Or not?' Some states were already dealing with this issue, but Carlson was getting calls from other states about what he was going to do. If these inmates were segregated, the director was aware that they were then pinpointed. Other inmates would confront them and possibly want to assault or kill them, thinking they might spread the disease.

According to Farkas, everyone sat down.

> We brought in our medical director. We talked with the Centers for Disease Control. We had many health service people go over it with us. It was Norm's ultimate decision to not separate them. Norm made absolutely the right decision.

Cubans in Prison. More than 100,000 Cubans came to the United States and were assimilated. The next issue was how to deal with the problematic Cubans who Fidel Castro had sent to the United States. Castro emptied his jails and mental hospitals and put these people on boats to Miami. There were 5,000 or more of them; they did not have paperwork or other identification. President Jimmy Carter decided to take them and put them in our jails and prisons. This created all types of problem. The Bureau of Prisons leaders had to decide several issues. "Do you separate them? Where do you place them? It was something no one wanted to deal with, but Norm knew that it was a presidential decision and he had to deal with it. So he faced it head on."[23]

Norm concentrated the Cubans in a few institutions; his logic was to keep them together. He also wanted to put them in facilities with Cuban interpreters in the community. The Federal Penitentiary at Atlanta received a large percentage of these Cuban prisoners, because of the number of Cuban interpreters in that community. In the short run, this strategy worked very well, but in the long run, the Cuban prisoners were the instigators of the major riot at the Federal Penitentiary at Atlanta in 1987 as a protest to the fact that they were scheduled to be returned to Cuba. However, in the late 1970s, when deciding on their placement, no one could have anticipated this.[24]

Deadly Fire at Federal Correctional Institution Danbury, Connecticut. Jerry Farkas, who was regional director at the time, tells how the fire at Federal Correctional Institution Danbury, in which five inmates were killed, was one of the lowest points of Carlson's career.

> Director Carlson went down there to support staff. He had a complete investigation made of what contributed to the fire; it was never uncovered who had started it. It was discovered that the doors were installed incorrectly so they would swing the wrong way. It was necessary to replace some of the tile in the bathrooms as part of routine maintenance, and some of it was not fire resistant.

Farkas reported "it was an embarrassment to the Bureau. Norm took the bull by the horns; we spent thousands, if not millions, to upgrade the safety of the facility and others around the system." Farkas was also impressed that five inmates lost their lives, and "Norm looked at it like we lost five human beings . . . . He took immediate action to insure against a similar incident happening again."[25]

The Warden and His Bathroom. Steve Schwalb, who was head of the Internal Affairs Unit for several years, told how in his mind "Norm is as good as I have ever seen, both in understanding and articulating the real essence of what the issue is, in everyday simple and humble type terms." He went on:

> I remember one of my staff investigating a warden using institutional money to build a bathroom in the warden's office. We learned that the bathroom had been built as alleged, and it turned out that the policy was followed and appropriate approvals had been secured. It was one of these things when the policy allowed a fair amount of latitude with the warden in terms of how to prioritize the use of certain types of funds. I reported to Norm that there was no technical violation of the policy. His comment was interesting, in that he said, "Well, I wonder what makes the warden think he couldn't have gone down the hall and used the bathroom that everyone else uses or as I do in the central office as the director." It was a rhetorical question that didn't need an answer, but he was asking what was this person thinking?[26]

Simplicity Will Do Just Fine, Thank You. Steve Schwalb, former head of internal affairs, cited another example. He said that "Norm had a way of challenging you in using fifty cent words when a five cent word would do." Schwalb said that he had "a staff person who was a little flowery with words." In this particular situation, a warden was accused of not placing the government decal on his car. Some alleged that he was driving the government vehicle on unofficial business. Yet, as it turned out, the warden did not want to drive the car with the decal on it in the urban setting where the prison was located. He felt that with the decals on it, he could very well get rocks or even bullets headed in his direction. We concurred that his not using government decals was a prudent thing to do.[27]

Schwalb went on:

> The guy on my staff who wrote the report said that, therefore, it is appropriate for the warden's car to be 'sans' decal. I got this note from Norm, who said, 'Steve, come see me.' I went in, and he said, 'What is this word?' Here is a guy with a master's degree and a very bright guy. How am I going to explain it? I don't want to be condescending, obviously. I said, 'It is a French word that means without.' And he said, 'Why don't we just say without?' That is Norm Carlson. What is this with the French? Why not the English? I also remember that Norm was an incredibly good writer. He used simple terms, nothing fancy or elaborate.[28]

Murders at Atlanta. Benjamin Civiletti, U.S. Attorney General at the time, further documented Carlson's style of leadership in handling situations. He said that he was reminded of an incident that showed Carlson's leadership:

> In Atlanta Penitentiary, we had twenty-one murders. The solution seems much simpler with hindsight than it was at the time. Norm was able to handle it by transferring the leaders of various ethnic or racial groups out of Atlanta so that they did not clash there. For instance, a Mexican gang, a black gang, or an Aryan Brotherhood gang, all of whom had leaders in the same penitentiary, were continually fighting each other. By transferring the leaders out, the murders seemed to stop, just as surprising as they had started a year before. That was a partial success story. It is tough to lose the twenty-one men. On the other hand, it was solved and corrected and did not continue endlessly."[29]

Significantly, what Norm did at Atlanta is a common practice today. State departments of corrections have been sending their troublemakers to the federal prison system for the past few decades, and state departments of corrections have been transferring gang members from one facility to another, to segregate gangs as much as possible from each other, for about the same amount of time.

Conclusions

Norman A. Carlson was an outstanding leader, as one interviewed former staff member after another has noted. Those outside the Bureau also saw him as one of the best leaders in government service. This chapter described some of Norm's principles of leadership, and it discussed the proactive learning culture in the Bureau. Finally, this chapter examined how Carlson handled a number of troubling situations and set a pattern for other correctional leaders to follow.

Endnotes

1. John Hurley sent this e-mail November 2005. Steve Martin was interviewed October 2005.

2. Pat Sledge indicated this in an interview in 2005.

3. Norm Carlson indicated this in an interview in July 2005.

4. Steve Grzegorek said this while interviewed August 2005.

5. Ibid.

6. Ibid.

7. A number of staff made this comment.

8. This, too, was a frequent response of staff.

9. Ibid.

10. Norm Carlson indicated this in an interview in July 2005.

11. Ibid.

12. Ibid.

13. Ibid.

14. Ibid.

15. Steve Grzegorek was interviewed August 2005.

16. Ibid.

17. John Hurley was interviewed November 2005.

18. Ibid.

19. Office of the Inspector General, "Select Application Control Review of the Federal Bureau of Prisons' SENTRY Database System," www.usdoj.gov/org/report/BOP/a0325/app8.htm (accessed July 26, 2009).

20. Steve Grzegorek was interviewed August 2005.

21. Ibid.

22. Jerry Farkas was interviewed October 2005.

23. Ibid.

24. Ibid.

25. Ibid.

26. Steve Schwalb was interviewed November 2005.

27. Ibid.

28. Ibid.

29. Benjamin Civiletti was interviewed January 2006.

Chapter 9

Innovations and Change

Norm was open to new initiatives. He would read the Executive Summary (not more than a page-and-a-half) of a proposal. If it seemed to make sense, a meeting was arranged with the Assistant Directors and others who would be affected by the change being proposed. Issues were raised, "kicked around," and a preliminary "go/ no go" decision reached. The next stop, if it were a "go" decision, was trying the idea as a pilot project. Timely follow-up reports were expected concerning the pilot project's preliminary and final results. Thus, while new ideas were welcomed, there was much scrutiny and careful evaluation built into their implementation. It was not an impossible "sell," but it clearly was far from anything goes.

Robert Levinson, Ph.D., former Deputy Assistant Director of Inmate Services, Bureau of Prisons[1]

Norman A. Carlson may have continued what was good about the Federal Bureau of Prisons, as previously suggested, but he used his management skills to make significant changes in the agency. Norm was an effective change agent for several reasons.

- He was not afraid of change and was willing to initiate a change if he felt it were the right thing to do.
- He was a calculated risk-taker and quite careful of the battles that he chose to fight and the resistance to change.

- He surrounded himself, both inside and outside the agency, with the brightest people he knew. He wanted the best information and insights that were available in evaluating the proposed innovation.
- He used the information he had obtained from his conversations and readings, as well as his keen intuition, to stay ahead of the curve. He simply understood what was coming better than his contemporaries, and this is what led to many of the innovations.
- Contributing to his effectiveness as a change agent was his credibility among the Attorney General's office and with Congress. Other directors of federal agencies would likely have encountered much more resistance to change than he did during the years he was director.

The innovations of the Carlson's years, discussed in this section, include professionalization of the agency; increased staff training; gender and racial integration of the agency; regionalization; expansion of unit management; innovative architectural design; establishment of the inmate grievance system; acceptance of the Bureau as a family; the development of an alternative model to institutionalization at Federal Correctional Institution Butner; establishment of the Office of Internal Affairs; experimentation with co-corrections (coeducational correctional facilities) as a means to more humanize prison facilities; and the hiring of ex-offenders as Bureau of Prisons' staff members. Some of these innovations had previously been developed by Carlson's predecessors and he expanded their use; others were totally new.

Professionalization of the Agency

Norm's vision of corrections as a profession was one of the earliest themes he articulated once he became director of the Bureau of Prisons.[2] Director James Bennett had previously focused on professionalization in the Federal Bureau of Prisons, and some state departments of corrections, such as Connecticut, Minnesota, and California, saw professionalization as a major part of their corrections mission.

Bob Matthews, former Bureau warden made this comment:

> He professionalized the agency. The directors since his tenure have built on his solid foundation of professionalism and high standards. The Bureau of Prisons still enjoys an excellent reputation with Congress, courts, and the Department of Justice because of Norm's uncompromising focus and credibility... I think that he did a lot to bring the Bureau of Prisons up to the level of the FBI in terms of reputation with Congress and the Justice Department.[3]

The first step in professionalizing the agency was to inform staff that he expected them to behave with integrity. He then proceeded to make a number of changes to professionalize the Bureau of Prisons. In Exhibit 9.1, Pete Earley, a former *Washington Post* reporter and author of many highly praised books, including one on the U.S. Penitentiary at Leavenworth, Kansas, aptly described the professionalism that Norm brought to the Bureau during the time that he was director.

Exhibit 9.1 Statement from Pete Earley on the Biggest Accomplishments of Norm's Career

"In my opinion, the biggest accomplishments of Norm's career—and there were several—was the professionalization of the federal Bureau of Prisons.... During the two years that I spent researching my book at Leavenworth USP, I never saw or heard of an inmate being abused. None. Later, I would spend time in the city jail in Miami, and I would discover that inmate abuse there was a daily happening. Treating inmates firmly, but with respect and without cruelty was Norm's mantra and he forced the entire system to change. It was not easy. It took tough minded determination. I remember him telling me once that the general public did not understand the purpose of prisons. It was NOT to punish inmates. The punishment was isolation from society. Therefore, it was not his employees' job to inflict pain or make inmates suffer. Norm simply would not accept any sadistic or cruel behavior, even during the worst of times when two of his officers were murdered in Marion. . . .

"Norm was responsible for insisting that the term 'guard' be dropped in favor of 'correctional officer' and with that title change, he demanded more from his officers. He introduced a dress code that did away with the old cop uniform with its badges and clubs. He had his junior officers wear blue blazers, white shirts, gray slacks, and ties. He understood that if his officers were going to be seen as professionals, they needed to dress and act accordingly.

"He raised the Bureau's overall expectations when it came to how prisons were operated. It wasn't enough simply to keep prisoners from going over the walls. Norm expected his prisons to be well running machines, freshly painted and spotless. In his mind, a clean prison was a sign of a well run facility. . . .

"In addition to instituting a dress code, Norm began a training program inside the Bureau of Prisons that further emphasized professionalism. He required his officers to move from one facility to another if they wished to be promoted up the ranks. This was important because it helped prevent 'kingdom' building and rivalry between institutions. It also promoted uniformity and it forced his managers to become more versatile. The once all-powerful wardens were replaced by multi-talented management teams."

Source: E-mail received November 28, 2005 and used with permission.

Emphasis on Staff Training

Norm also placed major emphasis on staff training. He believed that the training programs would be a way to make certain of the continuity and consistency in the Bureau's philosophy and expectations. He also was aware that staff training would be useful in breaking down the barriers existing between custody and treatment staff in correctional facilities. The number one priority of custody staff is to maintain a secure, escape-proof institution, while treatment staff are responsible for providing services to inmates. Custodial staff, especially in maximum-security facilities, often felt that treatment staff interfered with their role of maintaining a secure prison. There was sometimes open conflict between custody and treatment personnel.

In addition to using staff training to resolve the dichotomy between custody and treatment, Norm want to recognize the importance of the role of correctional officers, who would no longer be considered "guards" in the Federal Bureau of Prisons.[4] Norm extended this role change started by his predecessors throughout the agency.

Norm knew that he needed a "point person" to set up training, to propose curriculum, and to train those who would be the training officers. He heard about some training in the Atlanta Federal Penitentiary led by Sherman Day, Ph.D., a professor from Georgia State University. With his ever-sharp persuasion skills, he enlisted Sherman Day to develop training for the Bureau of Prisons. Professor Day took a two-year leave of absence from Georgia State University and came to work for the Bureau. Professor Day was a former director of the National Institute of Corrections and Assistant Director of the Bureau of Prisons. He summarizes what they accomplished in staff training:

> I'll go back to 1967 in the Atlanta Federal Penitentiary. I started going out there two nights a week to train the line staff in human relations skills. When Norm became Director in 1970, he made the decision he was going to control prisons. He knew that you're not going to be able to do it with sticks and guns, because eventually in riots the inmates end up with those sticks and guns. So, you're going to have to control it by the staff working with the inmates and being able to detect problems and being able to solve them before they happen. I think Norm found out about the program that seemed to be quite successful. So, he asked me to come to Washington to spend a year to develop those training programs throughout the Bureau. This was in the early 1970s.

I got to know Norm quite well, and we decided to establish training centers basically to train line staff. There had been an effort elsewhere in the nation to train correctional officers but not to the degree of teaching them Norm's philosophy of running prisons efficiently, effectively, and humanely. We had already started one before me, and then I started one in El Reno in the old warden's house. When I joined the Bureau, we expanded to regional centers, and helped develop a curriculum working with top staff at the Bureau. Norm wanted the curriculum to include what was essential to turn the Federal prison system into an effective, efficient, and humane prison system.[5]

When Sherman Day, Ph.D., returned to his teaching position at Georgia State University, Sam Samples, Ph.D., another of the early leaders of training in the Bureau, continued his work. Samples commented:

Norm was a great advocate of staff training and did more for that function than any person probably has before or since. He was very personally involved in the curricula, how we conducted ourselves, in the training we did, and so on. I was called up to see him regularly with questions and so forth.[6]

Implemented Gender and Racial Integration in the Bureau of Prisons

Bob Matthews a Bureau of Prisons warden, noted that "as an African American, the thing that impressed me about Norm was that he did a lot to advance equal opportunity in the Bureau. Norm selected the first African-American assistant director and regional director."[7] Matthews thought Attica had made a big impression on Norm. Norm was aware that most of the federal prisons, like state prisons, were in rural areas and staffed by whites, but with a large minority-inmate population. Not surprisingly, according to Matthews, you would have a lack of understanding and communication. He explained, "Norm recognized that you had to have at least some staff that looked like the people who were locked up. Norm moved ahead of the problem on this one, and, in my mind, he gets a lot of kudos for advancing equal opportunity hiring."[8]

Charlie Turnbo, former Bureau of Prisons' warden, also stated that Norm "was way ahead of the push on minorities."[9] According to Turnbo, Norm learned from an earlier riot where Hispanic prisoners took over the Federal Correctional Institution El Reno where not one staff member was a minority.[10] J. D. Williams, former Assistant Director and an African American, talked about how the Equal Employment Opportunity (EEO) program was initiated in the Bureau of Prisons:

> In the latter part of 1971, Dick Lyles and I became concerned about the lack of minority staff in the Bureau of Prisons' facilities. We composed a paper outlining those concerns and included recommendations to rectify the situation. Aware of the racial climate, we decided that if we followed proper protocol, our paper would never get to Norm, so . . . we delivered it directly to him!
>
> In those days, it wasn't fashionable to be pro-EEO and the Bureau was dominated by white males. However, Norm Carlson was extremely supportive and told us that we now needed to come up with a plan, implement it, and make it happen. And that was the beginning of the EEO program for the Bureau of Prisons.
>
> Norm Carlson always did what he thought was right, whether it was popular or not. And he wasn't interested in any personal gain when he made his decisions. He was raised a 'good ol' farm boy' and he had an inner strength or belief in doing the right thing. I believe this gave him great leadership abilities. [11]

Lee Jett, the first African-American warden, acknowledged Norm's strong affirmative action stance. "I had thought, and I still do think, that the Bureau's EEO program seems to be one of the best in the federal government, bar none." Jett noted, "Equal Opportunity would not have happened without Norm. He had the commitment that paid off. He had a personal interest in it." Jett added, "I'm thinking this is within this guy's heart. He believes this, and if he believes it, it's going to get done."[12]

J. D. Williams went on to tell how females began working in men's units in the Bureau of Prisons. He was warden at the San Diego Metropolitan Correctional Center (MCC), and it became necessary to assign female correctional officers to work on a floor that housed male prisoners. When the assistant director came to tour the facility, he noticed female officers working there and immediately informed the director. Norm asked him, "Are the inmates causing problems?"

The assistant director responded, "No!" Norm asked, "Is the unit clean?" The assistant director said, "Yes, but we don't place women in men's units." To which Norm responded, "Well, we're going to have to change that then." From that time on, women began working in men's units in the Bureau of Prisons.[13] In Exhibit 9.2 Margaret Hambrick, former Bureau of Prisons warden, related how Norm Carlson had an impact on her career.

Exhibit 9.2 Memories of Norm Carlson on the First Woman Warden's Career

"I met him in the Regional Office when he came through, but I am sure I came to his attention more through Jim Henderson. Anyway, after eighteen months, I was selected as Warden at Federal Correctional Institution Morgantown. This was a landmark decision. I was the first woman to be warden of an all-male prison—minimum security though it was. That must have taken courage on Norm's part. He (and Jim) were betting a lot on my ability to succeed. I was also only twenty-nine and the youngest warden ever appointed.

"For me it was extremely hard. I had never been an associate warden (except for a three-month acting stint at Alderson) and that is the training ground for being warden. I am sure my appointment caused uproar in the AW [assistant warden] ranks. There were all those qualified males out there, and he went over them and selected a woman who had never been an AW. It was the Carter years when promoting women became important, so I think my appointment served the Bureau well. As I recall, he made a somewhat controversial regional director appointment at the same time. One person told me I was taking the heat because others were afraid to complain about the RD [regional director]."

Source: E-mail received in November 2005 and used with permission.

The annual report at the time that Carlson retired announced that "minorities and women now head four major institutions and hold assistant warden positions in four others."[14] Norm's stance on affirmative action was way ahead of the game. He knew the importance of affirmative action because of the riots and collective disorders in state prisons and in the one federal facility in Oklahoma. Yet, he moved on the employment of minorities and women before it was required of him by federal law, because it was the right thing to do. It was another example of his risk-taking, but he did so in a politically savvy way.

Implemented Regionalization

By 1972, there was a widespread concern that the organization and supervision of the entire Bureau was too much for a single person to do. It was not long before there was discussion about regionalization. Bureau staff examined several regionalized agencies. Norm supported the notion of dividing the Bureau into five regions, which was later amended to six. A regional director in charge of each region would report to the director. As part of the regionalization process, regional directors would meet every quarter with Norm to generate policies and operations throughout the Bureau.

David Jelinek, associate commissioner of the Bureau of Prisons, commented on these planning retreats:

> When he first became director, he felt he had to be decisive. He didn't want to talk about problems or issues that much; he just wanted to make decisions. When we started having retreats to consider the issue of regionalization, we liked the results. Norm learned that you don't have to short circuit the decision-making process. We were really operating almost like a Quaker meeting. As I indicated in my memoirs, these meetings were one of the most satisfying and fulfilling experiences of my life. We had detailed agendas, with advanced papers to study, and we arm wrestled the forty items or so on the agenda. I think they are still doing it, and I can't think of a better way to operate a complex, nationwide agency.[15]

With this innovation of regionalization, it became possible to manage what could have been a totally unwieldy organizational structure. During the process of regionalization, Norm Carlson changed his approach to meetings. Until that point, he was known as a stickler for precision, terseness, and timeliness, but he found that it was functional for the agency to permit the regional directors and assistant directors to hammer out policy and issues facing the regionalization process and the Bureau's many other concerns.

Expanded Unit Management

As mentioned in Chapter 3, unit management, (developed by Robert Levinson, Ph.D., and staff[16] and sometimes called "functional units") divides the prison into small units. Roy Gerard maintains: "Unit management is an approach to inmate and institutional management designed to improve control and relationships by dividing a large institution population into smaller, more manageable groups, to improve the delivery of correctional services."[17] The unit, in some sense, becomes a prison unto itself. The origins of unit management go back to the 1960s, but only a few institutions used it. During the time that Carlson served as Director, unit management expanded throughout the Bureau.

Unit management combines the roles of the correctional officer and caseworker. This collapses the age-old conflict between the security and treatment roles. Unit management actually ties into the professionalization and decentralization movement, which was already present in the Bureau. The rationale behind the unit management organizational structure is twofold: (1) decentralizing authority in the institution will ensure maximum services to inmates, (2) dividing the prison into small units will ensure better control of inmates.[18]

One of the most succinct definitions of unit management was on the wall of the superintendent's office in the Alaska Department of Corrections' Palmer Prison: "Unit Management is not a program, it's a better way to manage programs."[19] Lee Jett, former Bureau of Prisons warden, added, "I think unit management worked so much better for the inmates because generally they could get responses to inquiries right away."[20]

Unit management, one of the innovations that expanded during the time that Norman Carlson was director, has had a wide effect on corrections. As one federal institution after the other, including the Bureau of Prisons penitentiaries, implemented unit management, it also started to be used in state prisons.

Sought Innovative Architectural Design

After Norm was named director of the Bureau in 1970, he became aware that the Bureau would be facing an incredible explosion of inmates and that it would be necessary to build a number of new facilities. According to Dr. Walter Menninger, of the Menninger Clinic, "He didn't want a cookie cutter traditional model." Dr. Menninger then related Carlson's plan to avoid a traditional design:

> Somehow he got me on the list and invited me to be part of the facilities' planning group, with Gary Mote and others. What was exciting is that with most advisory groups, the agency views the group as a pain. Norm really structured it so that the input of the advisory group was sought and listened

to. The next meeting things were changed because of the comments.

Dr. Menninger tells how serious Norm was in terms of having a meaningful design:

> Norm got the architects and planners together and flew them to various spots in the country to look at existing prisons. He even had them come to the Menninger clinic where I visited with them about some of the psychological aspects of the correctional population. It was most gratifying to be in a position where your opinions were respected and, where relevant, would be applied. [21]

William Patrick, a member of this architectural team headed by Assistant Director Gary Mote, reported in Exhibit 9.3 how form follows function—how the new designs followed the approach that was needed to administer the correctional function of these facilities.

Exhibit 9.3 Form Follows Function

"We started at that time with what we thought was a major building program. We had about half a dozen institutions to build. We had to make personal presentations to Norm as director so he got to review the plans for the new facilities. So, I got to know Norm fairly well because at that time, he would have these relatively informal sessions and, of course, in doing it, we got to understand Norm's view of corrections, treatment of inmates, and treatment of staff. Like most of the staff, I thought Norm was wonderful, still do, and I think that he is one of the greatest guys who ever lived. He was just an outstanding director.

"One of the things he believed is that you did not separate staff and inmates. Another of his beliefs was that that the way to get inmates to act the way you want them to act is to treat them like human beings. He also wanted to normalize, as much as possible, the correctional facilities, and finally, he wanted the facilities to be secure.

"He had us design housing units which were very normal—even had wooden doors. The cells were not called cells but 'rooms.' And they looked like rooms; they looked like Y.M.C.A. rooms. At the same time, you had to take care of those things that were critical, such as visual supervision, so staff walking around the unit could interact with inmates while maintaining good visual supervision throughout the unit. You tried, as much as possible, to come up with housing units that attained this ideal. We had some interesting triangular-shaped pods come up. Over the past thirty years, these architectural forms have come up as the model for all kinds of correctional facilities.

"Again, this was part of Norm's vision that staff and inmates should not be separated by bars and staff should intermingle with inmates. That brought about certain things that were different. Among other things, this manifested itself in the construction of the housing unit and the rest of the institution. The dining room didn't have the shotgun tower in the center as in some states, like that present at Stateville, Illinois. In fact, the staff in the institution was not armed. There was no need for inmates to hurt staff because they were not going to get weapons by doing so."

Source: Interviewed October 2005.

The function of these architectural forms was to express Norm's understanding of the vision of corrections. Director Bennett had previously initiated some of these changes, such as taking weapons out of the prison, but Carlson expanded his vision of what a prison should look like and how it should function. This was a vision that he reiterated every time he had an opportunity—in talking with wardens at wardens' conferences, in speaking on the Hill, and in interacting with staff. As Patrick notes,

> After working for the Bureau of Prisons for a few months, you knew Norm's vision so well, that Norm could send you for a meeting with a Congressman or Senator or director of

some agency, which he often did, and you could speak for the Bureau because you knew exactly how Norm would have answered most questions.[22]

Patrick recalls how a high-powered warden of another federal institution became superintendent of a new federal jail. Patrick was showing him how the visiting room would be laid out where the family, inmates, and staff would be intermingling. He reacted, "You can't let them intermingle and touch each other." And then went on to say that Norm was wrong, and he was certain he would see it his way." He took the architectural designs to Norm and told him he was wrong. Norm responded, "I am not wrong. Mr. Patrick has that exactly the way I want it. He had to come back to me and said that [my way] was the way it was supposed to be."[23]

Thus, the significance of the new federal facilities was far more than they looked different than traditional prisons, which they did. They illustrated a more humane way of treating inmates by providing a more normalizing environment in which incarceration could occur.

Developed the Inmate Grievance System

In an interview conducted with Norman Carlson on November 30, 1989, as part of the Oral History Project—which consisted of interviews conducted with previous directors—Carlson talked about the inmate grievance process as part of the humane treatment of inmates.

Exhibit 9.4 Norman Carlson's Comments about the Inmate Grievance System

"One [example of humane treatment] is the development of the Inmate Grievance system, a program that was one of the first of its kind in the United States. That system had its origins in a meeting I attended during the early 1970s with judges on the Eighth Circuit Court of Appeals in St. Louis. The judges asked me to attend the meeting, as they were discussing the tremendous number of lawsuits being filed by inmates from the Federal Medical Center in Springfield, Missouri. Court dockets were overwhelmed with inmate complaints, many of which concerned such trivial matters as ill-fitting shoes and breakfast cereal that was cold. The judges asked if there was some way that we in the Bureau of Prisons could resolve these and similar issues before they reached the court and further clogged the dockets.

"When I returned to Washington, I met with Gene Barkin, Clair Cripe, and Ira Kirschbaum of our legal staff to see if we could devise a mechanism that would assist the courts in resolving inmate complaints. They came up with the notion of developing an administrative remedy process, which we first piloted at Springfield. Based on the success of that endeavor, the system was soon expanded to all institutions. Today, virtually every correctional agency in the United States has implemented a grievance mechanism modeled on the Bureau's program.

"In my opinion, what made the grievance mechanism a success is the fact that it has credibility with the courts as well as with most inmates. Judges and inmates recognize that when there are legitimate complaints, the Bureau will take steps to correct the problems before they become issues for the courts."

Source: Excerpt from interview conducted as part of the Bureau of Prisons' Oral History Project, Springfield, Missouri, November 30, 1989, quoted in *Federal Prison Journal 1* (Summer 1990), pp. 39-40.

As part of his vision of a humane prison, Carlson strongly held that inmates must be provided with their constitutionally required rights. At the same time, with his always present regard for the federal courts, Norm wanted to come up with a procedure to expedite the courts' handling of what seemed to be impossible caseloads from federal correctional institutions, often of a trivial or minor nature. Shortly after they began in the Federal Bureau of Prisons, such inmate grievance procedures became part of every state department of corrections.

Envisioned the Bureau as a Family

Gil Ingram, one of the assistant directors of the Bureau of Prisons, commented that "Norm developed and nurtured the concept of the Bureau of Prisons' Family without highlighting it in writing."[24] Charlie Turnbo, a former Bureau of Prisons' warden, added, "He made the Bureau into a family-like environment. From the newest correctional officer to those in executive positions, they all felt a part of the Bureau-family."[25] David C. Jelinek, associate commissioner of the Bureau of Prisons, noted: "I found the 'small pond' of the Bureau much more to my liking than the huge and highly politicized Department of State," where he had worked before.

> The Bureau people took great pride in considering themselves 'a family,' a view that was not unwarranted. Most people were on a first-name basis, and a long-standing policy of requiring supervisors and managers to transfer from institution to institution when being promoted helped counter the natural tendency for local units to diverge and distance themselves from other units.[26]

The Bureau was much smaller in terms of institutions and staff than it would be in the late 1980s and 1990s, and this made the family-life feeling a more realistic goal. The frequent social get-togethers conducted by the Bureau also enhanced this feeling. Norm did his part in promoting this family atmosphere by knowing the names of staff of all levels in the institutions, by responding to death in staff's families by sending a sympathy note, and by doing everything possible to comfort and provide support to those families who lost members in the line of duty.

Supported the Experiment at Federal Correctional Institution Butner

The Bureau decided to build a new approach to classification and programming concepts at a new facility under construction in Butner, North Carolina. This facility was unique in several ways. It was the first adult male institution built for unit management that included a campus-style plan without armed gun towers. As part of its mission, it was to develop and test new correctional concepts—including the theory of imprisonment and inmate programming developed by Norval Morris. This model was designed to eliminate the coercive aspects of rehabilitation programming implicitly contained in the medical model.

Norval Morris' 1975 book, *The Future of Imprisonment*, argued that coupling release from incarceration with prison program achievement was both ineffective and coercive. It was coercive because inmates would do virtually anything to gain an early release, and accordingly was ineffective because it fostered "shamming"—telling staff and the parole board whatever it is they want to hear. Morris advocated disconnecting release readiness from program performance.[27]

Morris' model had four components:

1. Self-help programs must be offered but could not be required.
2. Inmates must have a predetermined length of stay during institutional placements.
3. Prison programs must include a gradual testing of inmates' suitability for release.
4. The general pattern of living within the facility should be as similar as possible to the ordinary working of an individual in the community.[28]

Levinson added seven key elements to the Bureau's implementation of this approach:

1. Establishment of a humane and secure environment
2. Random selection of "deep-end" [or long-term, recidivist] prisoners
3. Voluntary program participation (inmates could "opt-out" after a ninety-day trial period)
4. A graduated release plan
5. A fixed-release date for prisoners
6. Program evaluation conducted by an independent evaluation group
7. Measures of success that included both in-house and post-release behavior[29]

Operation of Butner's programs also resulted in considerable negative media reactions and from both liberal and conservative communities. For liberals, Butner was "brain-washing inmates"; for conservatives, Butner was "coddling inmates" and the system needed to "get tough" with them. The Research Triangle evaluation of this facility showed some positive effects, but it did reveal that Norm was open to Morris' ideas, as he was open to new ideas from other academic criminologists.[30]

Established the Office of Internal Affairs

In 1978, Norm decided to establish the Office of Internal Affairs. The purpose of this office was to avoid, as much as possible, corruption and abuses within the system. Steve Schwalb, who was the third chief of the Internal Affairs Office from January of 1981 to October of 1983, reported:

> The chief reported directly to the director, which I thought was indicative of his view of how important this office needed to be and how independent it needed to be. So, irrespective of where the allegations came in the organization,

no one could say, 'The investigation was less than fully independent.'[31]

At the same time we had a centralized approach to an audit policy in those days. Audits were done in the regional offices but the overall policy oversight was in the Internal Affairs office. This was indicative of Norm's belief that you had to present, both internally and externally, an image of an agency that set high standards, whether it was doing internal audits or misconduct investigations.[32]

Schwalb explained, "We had some complex, serious, and challenging investigations during my tenure, and with Norm's support, we worked through them. We collaborated at times with the FBI and other agencies and so some of them were pretty harried investigations."[33]

Schwalb told of one investigation in the Federal Correctional Institution Terminal Island, California, in which fifty-one staff members were accused of different things. He stayed out there for weeks. Some senior staff were found guilty and ended up going to prison themselves. They introduced contraband in the facility, had sex with inmates, and had been involved in taking inmates out for furloughs with their wives.[34]

However, the Internal Affairs Unit, as is true of police organizations, was in conflict from time to time. Some external accusations accused the Internal Affairs Unit in particular cases of exempting certain staff from guilty findings when they were, in fact, guilty. Staff held differing opinions of how Internal Affairs had handled a particular case. At other times, the higher administration, perhaps even extending to Norm, were reported to be unhappy with the findings of the Internal Affairs Unit concerning a highly popular individual in the Bureau of Prisons. Yet, the fact still remains, regardless of how reasonable individuals may disagree from time to time on how a particular case or incident ought to be handled, the Internal Affairs Unit was a pivotal innovation that maintained the high standards of integrity in the Bureau of Prisons.

Established Co-Corrections Facilities

The first co-educational institutions, known among corrections practitioners as co-correctional, opened in 1971. The purpose of these facilities was to create a more normal environment and to reduce some of the pains of imprisonment. The Federal Bureau of Prisons opened five of these facilities in the 1970s—Federal Correctional Institution Fort Worth (1971), Federal Correctional Institution Morgantown (1971), Federal Correctional Institution Lexington (1974), Federal Correctional Institution Pleasanton (1974), and Federal Correctional Institution Terminal Island (1975). All but Federal Correctional Institution Lexington were phased out in the next decade. As Charlie Turnbo, former Bureau of Prisons' warden, reported, "One disappointment to Norm was co-corrections. I was warden of two facilities that were co-correctional. It was a worthy experience, but overcrowding and other things simply defeated it."[35]

Hired Ex-Offenders

Another promising innovation that did not prove to be lasting was the hiring of ex-offenders. Norm hired several ex-offenders in the 1970s, the majority of whom did well and some of whom had quite a successful career in the Bureau of Prisons. Yet, the political climate of the 1980s, with new legal norms, precluded the continued hiring of ex-offenders.

Conclusions

The innovations discussed in this chapter proved to be major paradigm shifts in the Bureau of Prisons. Federal agencies are legendary for resisting change, but Carlson made many important changes during the seventeen years he was director. These paradigm shifts demonstrated the significance of Norman Carlson's leadership.

The question must be raised: Why did he succeed? Rob Goffee and Gareth Jones' *Why Should Anyone Be Led by You?* suggest that leaders who are successful innovators know when to challenge the norms and when to conform. They rarely, according to Goffee and

Jones, challenge all the norms at once. They do not move ahead on the change process until they understand the organizational context.[36]

The fact is that Director Carlson was an extremely shrewd change agent. He kept ahead of the curve, was always well informed, had the loyalty of staff throughout the organization, had credibility with and continued support from the Attorney General's Office and Congress, and showed good judgment when it was necessary to make organizational changes. And, if an innovation did not work or proved to be problematic, he knew when to pull the plug and back away from it.

Endnotes

1. Robert Levinson, Ph.D., made this comment in an e-mail August 2005.

2. Norm Carlson said this during an interview August 2005.

3. Bob Matthews was interviewed October 2005.

4. Support for the term "correctional officer" was adopted in an ACA policy on January 20, 1999. The policy has been re-ratified several times and continues in effect today. See www.aca.org/government/policyresolution

5. Sherman Day, Ph.D., was interviewed 2005.

6. Sam Samples, Ph.D., was interviewed November 2005.

7. Bob Matthews was interviewed October 2005.

8. Ibid.

9. Charlie Turnbo was interviewed October 2005.

10. Ibid.

11. J. D. Williams was interviewed October 2005.

12. Lee Jett was interviewed November 2005.

13. J. D. Williams was interviewed October 2005.

14. Norm Carlson reported this during an interview in August 2005.

15. David Jelinek was interviewed September 2005.

16. *See* his book: *Unit Management in Prisons and Jails*, 1999. American Correctional Association: Lanham, Maryland (Out of Print).

17. Roy Gerard said this in an e-mail August 2005.

18. *See* Robert B. Levinson and Roy E. Gerard. 1973. "Functional Units: A Different Correctional Approach," *Federal Probation 37*, December, pp. 8-16.

19. Cited in John W. Roberts. 1992. "Interview: Lee Jett," *Federal Prison Journal 3*, Fall, p. 55.

20. Lee Jett was interviewed November 2005.

21. Dr. Walter Menninger was interviewed November 2005.

22. William Patrick was interviewed October 2005.

23. Ibid.

24. Gil Ingram's e-mail received August 2005.

25. Charlie Turnbo was interviewed October 2005.

26. Memoirs of David C. Jelinek for family members, sent to author, pp. 125-27.

27. Norval Morris. 1975. *The Future of Imprisonment*. Chicago: University of Chicago Press.

28. Ibid.

29. Cited in Robert B. Levinson. 1994. "The Development of Classification and Programming," in *Escaping Prison Myths: Selected Topics in the History of Federal Corrections*, edited by John W. Roberts. Washington, D.C.: The American University Press, p. 101.

30. Robert B. Levinson and Donald A. Deppe. 1976. "Optional Programming: A Model Structure for the Federal Correctional Institution at Butner." *Federal Probation 40*, pp. 37-44.

31. Steve Schwalb was interviewed October 2005.

32. Ibid.

33. Ibid.

34. Ibid.

35. Charlie Turnbo was interviewed October 2005.

36. Rob Goffee and Gareth Jones. 2006. *Why Should Anyone Be Led by You? What It Takes To Be an Authentic Leader*. Boston, Massachusetts: Harvard Business School, pp. 109-110.

Chapter 10

Ripples of Norman Carlson's Leadership

Norm is what I have always considered the very best manager in the government. I was in the criminal division of the Department of Justice, and I was exposed to many, many agencies. None equaled Norm and his management of the Bureau of Prisons. His strength was not only in knowledge, which was there, but in his approach to issues which would come up when the Bureau of Prisons had made a mistake or had problems. He was always honest. His integrity carried him right through Congressional hearings and departmental inquiries. Whatever Norm said, people knew it was so, and he was very quick to say "I made a mistake," if that was the case.

Gerald Shur,[1] a career prosecutor with the Criminal Division in the Department of Justice. Shur is known as the "Father of WITSEC."

A major emphasis of this part of the book has been to portray how Norman A. Carlson created paradigm shifts in the Bureau of Prisons and, in fact, influenced a good agency to become a better agency. This chapter examines the wider context of Carlson's influence and explores the ripples his leadership created. Some of the most exciting ripples included:

- The effect of his influence and the positive direction of his leadership in developing programs and instituting training as well as

serving as moral compass through the 1970s and 1980s for state correctional agencies
- The strong support for the accreditation movement of the American Correctional Association
- The development and promotion of the National Institute of Corrections (NIC)
- The support for the Sentencing Institutes with federal judges, which began with former Director James Bennett
- The allocation of sufficient resources for the Bureau through the credibility and skill of Carlson's leadership in Congress and the Justice Department
- Establishment of the Federal Witness Protection Program (WITSEC) within the Bureau of Prisons, and the support for the covert activity that took place from the WITSEC program to the community
- Expansion of the Prison Fellowship movement into the Bureau of Prisons
- Sponsor of university research
- Support for internship programs, including the special relationships with Kent State University in Ohio and Gustavus Adolphus College in Minnesota

All of these items, which we will discuss in further detail, reveal the effects of Carlson's leadership in corrections and the criminal justice system.

The Stablizing Influence and Positive Direction of Carlson's Leadership for Corrections in the 1970s and 1980s

Anthony "Tony" Travisono, former executive director of the American Correctional Association, noted in an interview: "Norm believed in the ACA and was always actively involved in the activities of the Association."[2] Carlson was so involved that he was elected the President of the American Correctional Association from 1978-1980.

Travisono went on:
> Most directors in the 1970s, coping with the turmoil in corrections, turned to the Bureau of Prisons for help, strategy, and leadership. They especially turned to Norm where there was a need to transfer prisoners and gang leaders. When I was director of corrections, I transferred half a dozen prisoners or more from Rhode Island, to quiet down our institutions. State directors of corrections were able to move troublemakers around the federal prison system. Norm never refused any colleague trying to keep the peace.[3]

Don Yeomans, commissioner of the Correctional Service of Canada (CSC) from 1977 to 1985, tells in Exhibit 10:1 how the assistance of Norm Carlson helped corrections in Canada, which wanted a treaty with the Federal Bureau of Prisons to exchange prisoners.

Exhibit 10.1 Assistance to Corrections in Canada

"In 1977, I was appointed the Commissioner of the CSC [Correctional Service of Canada] without ever having been inside a prison. My appointment followed a series of very bad riots and a Parliamentary inquiry. I was told that I was being put in the job because of my managerial skills. Since my predecessor had died before my appointment, I searched for persons to whom I could turn for advice. One of the most valued sources was Norm Carlson who was the Director of the Bureau of Prisons at the time.

"I visited him in Washington, and he very generously took me to visit a number of his institutions. I learned about discipline, institution management, his strict insistence on institutional cleanliness, and watched carefully his excellent style of leadership.

"One of his suggestions really surprised me. He suggested that I take my wife with me from time to time when I visited the institutions. He took his wife with him and found that her presence enhanced communications with inmates and staff. I did so with increasing frequency, and it had the same effect. I was always very grateful for that unusual advice. As a result of our warm friendship (which continues to this day), CSC staff and Bureau staff visited each other's institutions regularly to exchange ideas.

"A very special project on which we worked together was the implementation of the International Transfer of Offenders. This was an excellent program promoted by the United Nations whereby persons convicted of an offence in one country could serve the sentence in their home country. The implementation of this legislation was complex because in the United States it meant ratification by a majority of the States. The Bureau and United States Department of Justice worked diligently on the project and the legislation was finally ratified. It was much simpler in Canada because only the Federal Government was involved.

"Finally the day came for the first transfer. American offenders in Canadian penitentiaries were gathered in a penitentiary in Kingston, Ontario and the Bureau gathered theirs in Chicago. According to my diary, Norm flew to Ottawa on Wednesday, October 11, 1978 and then we drove to Kingston. Somehow we got to Chicago together, because I distinctly remember standing on the tarmac in Chicago with him watching the Americans being unloaded and Canadians being loaded on a chartered aircraft. That was on Thursday, October 12, 1978. Those transfers have been going on as required ever since."

Source: E-mail received January 2, 2006.

Supported Accreditation Standards

Perhaps Norman Carlson's biggest contribution to American corrections is the role he played in the development of American Correctional Association standards for accreditation of correctional facilities. Tony Travisono commented on Norm's role:

> Norm was very instrumental in developing the standards that I have characterized as the most significant and major part of the American Correctional Association's (ACA)

influence on corrections since its inception in 1870. . . . The standards were something that the Association and its supporters had always dreamed about. We had suggested guidelines even back to the 1950s, but in the 1970s, the Association was willing to step forward with developing significant voluntary standards.[4]

Travisono went on to say that in 1976 there was a meeting concerning some controversial standards.

> Respected state directors and officers representing the warden's association had a major confrontation regarding certain standards. Norm was present and extremely influential in finding a compromise. The group was determined to stay at the meeting until the difference was resolved. Thanks to Norm and several others, agreements were reached.[5]

When Norm became president of the ACA (1978-1980), according to Travisono, "he became our man in the federal government." Griffin Bell, the Attorney General at the time, and his staff, wanted to write federal standards and not acknowledge the voluntary standards developed by the Association. Travisono continued:

> Of course, the Association was opposed to that idea. The Association was doing a good job in making the standards reasonable and acceptable. The association felt that if correctional departments were mandated to adopt the federal standards at a certain time, it would be difficult for states to comply. The Association was able to convince Attorney General Bell and his staff to think about the ramifications of such an act.

> Fortunately, when Benjamin Civiletti became Attorney General, he and Norm became very close, and we were able to get Civiletti to back off from the idea of the federal standards. He

agreed that the ACA was doing a good job, and that he was willing to accept our voluntary standards. That was certainly a big break for ACA and the concept of voluntary standards.

To my knowledge, no one since then has thought of bringing standards under federal control. I give Norm a great deal of credence for working with Civiletti and convincing him that the Association would be trusted. Of course, it helped a great deal that he was president of ACA at the time.[6]

Started Training Through the National Institute of Corrections (NIC)

The National Institute of Corrections was created in 1974 to provide training for state and local correctional administrators. Richard "Pete" Velde, (the head of the Law Enforcement Assistance Administration [LEAA]) at the time, and Norm worked together to create this project. LEAA money funded it and the Bureau of Prisons staffed it.[7]

Up until that point, very few correctional administrators had received any management training. The University of Chicago, with Norval Morris' leadership, as well as Long Beach State University in California, was involved in creating the initial curriculum. Later, the Wharton School of Business at the University of Pennsylvania and the University of Southern California participated in this project of training federal, state, and local administrators in both institutions and community-based corrections.[8]

Bill Wilkey, who started working with the National Institute of Corrections even before the legislation created this project, stated:

> Norm has been the most consistent force of the organization [NIC]. Even before the legislation, Norm volunteered the staff to run the organization. Then, once the legislation came, it was housed in the Bureau of Prisons.[9]

Dr. Walter Menninger, of the Menninger Clinic, became a member of the Board of the National Institue of Corrections, and he eventually served as chair for two terms. He also commented on Norm's importance to the National Institue of Corrections: "NIC was independent of the Bureau at the time, but the Bureau was a major source of support. Subsequently, it was enfolded under the Bureau. It was Norm's tempering of it along the way that carried it along."[10]

Norm Carlson continued his association with National Institue of Corrections following his retirement from the Bureau of Prisons and continues to be involved on the Advisory Board of Directors. The training programs of National Institue of Corrections have expanded, including the provision of management and specialty training for staff of state and local corrections throughout the United States. The National Institue of Corrections also provides training for juvenile justice and military corrections personnel through interagency agreements. The National Institue of Corrections provides classroom-based, broadcast, and online-training opportunities. In most training programs, participants develop individual action plans or initiate projects to implement in their agencies; in some cases, technical assistance may be available to help them carry out their action plans.[11]

Federal Judiciary and the Sentencing Institutes

U.S. District Judge Paul Magnuson defines Norm's relationship with the federal courts in the following way:

> Norm had an absolute policy for putting his best foot forward with the courts. Judges were strongly encouraged to visit institutions. Wardens were strongly encouraged to have good personal relationships with the judges. If a judge raised a concern, the warden was expected to deal with that concern. If it's an unfounded kind of thing, the warden was to deal with it seriously and show the judge why it's unfounded. There are a lot of hay stacks that don't have needles. If you happen to get one of those needles in a haystack, the warden was to deal with it.

The result of all this was that the Bureau and the courts really enjoyed a good working relationship. It has changed and I think it has changed in part because the Bureau has become a huge bureaucracy. I don't know a single warden in the Bureau of Prisons today. When Norm was director, I knew almost all of the wardens.[12]

Judge Magnuson defined Norm's role in the Sentencing Institutes. Sentencing Institutes were a combined effort of the probation department, the Federal Judicial Center, and the Bureau of Prisons. Norm usually attended their meetings. The Sentencing Institutes would bring a large group of judges from a certain circuit to a community that had a federal prison, and for a two or three days they would talk about sentencing policy, probation work, and the work of the Bureau of Prisons. The judges also had an opportunity to visit the prison and to sit down in small groups with inmates, which would be helpful in hearing the thought processes of inmates and what they were doing.[13]

Exhibit 10.2 shows U.S. Circuit Court of Appeals Judge Gerald Tjoflat's expanded statement about the Sentencing Institutes:

Exhibit 10.2 The Sentencing Institutes

"I first became acquainted with Norm Carlson, shortly after I went on the Federal district court in 1970. I came on in October and I think he was already director, but not long. In 1972, the chief justice appointed me as chair to the Judicial Conference to the United States Committee on the Administration and Probation System. . . . That was a seven-judge committee. It was charged with overseeing the probation and parole officers for the judiciary. It was also charged with putting on Sentencing Institutes in prisons. In those days, if you recall, we had indeterminate sentencing.

"I think the first meeting I attended of the committee, Judge Van Duzen of The Third Circuit was the chair. He turned to me and said, 'Judge Tjoflat, SI [a bill in Congress] had just been introduced in the

Senate.' That was the first bill that intended to reform the criminal code. What I recall is that the front part had to do with the substance of the criminal law and the back part had to do with corrections and sentencing and everything else. And I was in charge of monitoring the evolution of sentencing reform, which was the back part of the code.

"Anyhow, I got deeply involved in the task, and I remained on the committee until after Chief Justice Rehnquist reorganized the judicial conference of the United States. The last ten years I was on the committee, I was probably the chair. Before that, I did a lot of testifying before the House and Senate Judiciary Committees.

"I was involved with Norm Carlson because we put on Sentencing Institutes all over the country. I think we tried to get to every circuit about every three years at the most, more often than that, if possible. The Judiciary was small in those days by comparison to today. So, we would combine circuits with these Institutes. For example, we would combine the Ninth sometimes with the Tenth, the Eighth, and maybe the Seventh, and the Fourth, and the Fifth.

"The committee of the Judicial Conference would propose an Institute and the Conference would approve it. It was my job, so I would get together with the chief judges of the affected circuits and get agreements from them. We would get Judicial Conference approval and then decide where we were going to have it. We would have it in the city or a location very close to a federal prison. For example, like Lompoc in California, we would have the conference in Santa Barbara. Or, we would meet in Dallas or Fort Worth, because there were two facilities there, one in Dallas and one in Fort Worth. . . .

"These Institutes would last about three days, and we would have academics and statisticians, and all kinds of speakers having to do with crime and punishment. Then, we would visit the institution for a whole day. In getting ready to do that, I would meet with Norm ahead of time and would go to an institution. We would pick out some inmates who would 'rap with the judges.'

"Norm would be present for all of the Institutes. He and I would go to these places ahead of time. I can remember being with Norm Carlson in San Francisco at San Quentin. I can also recall going with him to the institution near Oakland that at the time had all the women. I can remember going with Al Wallenberg and Norm to Alcatraz a couple of times. God knows how many places I went with Carlson over that period of time.

"Between the Advisory Corrections Council and the Committee on Administration and Probation Systems and doing these Sentencing Institutes, we were forever interacting with Norm in terms of program, prison industry, and everything else you can imagine. He was still Director of the Bureau when I stepped out as chair of the committee."

Source: Interviewed October 2005

The Sentencing Institutes began before Carlson became director, but his strong support gave the Institutes such impetus and momentum. Norman Carlson courted federal judges, and they, in turn, responded to his leadership with great enthusiasm. Federal judges might call the Bureau's central office and ask for advice on sentencing questions for inmates. This, of course, was not appropriate, but it reflects the influence that Carlson had with the federal judiciary.

Leadership on the Hill

As good as Norm was with the federal judiciary, he was equally, if not, more effective in testifying before Congress and its subcommittees. Even before he became Director of the Bureau in 1970, he interacted with members of Congress. As David C. Jelinek, former Bureau official explained: "He was the director's man on the Hill; he cultivated a relationship with Congressmen and Senators, and the judges who were important on the Hill. He really understood the importance of that connection."[14]

Peter Bensinger, former Assistant Attorney General, put it this way:

> Norm testified very effectively with Congress, in terms of appropriations, in terms of programs, in terms of new facilities, and in terms of the needs of the department. Norm was

really one of the best witnesses you can find. He did not get defensive. He was usually backed by very clear and accurate facts. Even if there were issues, whether it was the rate of recidivism or an occurrence that might not have been anticipated, Norm could explain this in very real terms to people who sat on the appropriation committee. So, he was considered by Congress as a very well respected Federal officer. This was not a guy trying to make points at their expense. I also know that he was viewed as bipartisan, non-political.[15]

Wade Houk, an assistant director of the Bureau of Prisons who worked closely with Norm for a number of years, said that "Norm was, in my opinion, the best possible kind of witness in Congressional hearings. He understood this was not the place for him to extol the virtues of the Bureau of Prisons. This was the member's show."

Houk explained that, when members of Congress "asked Norm questions, he responded with short, concise, and accurate answers. So many others, including very senior executive branch officials, forgot this principle."[16]

Pete Earley, a reporter for the *Washington Post* and the author of several best-selling books, proposed that:

> Norm used the trust and friendships that he had gained in Congress to thwart attempts by the White House to appoint new directors and he lobbied hard even after he retired to keep the Bureau of Prisons in the hands of professionals who had risen up through the system.[17]

Interviewees reported a number of times Norman Carlson stood up to irate members of Congress, who usually wanted special treatment for those from their districts or states. Dr. Robert Brutsche, the Bureau's chief medical officer, reported that he and Norm met with the Congressmen and Senators from a particular state over the sentencing of a very important man from that state. They wanted to know what was going to happen and if there was any way the Bureau could have him placed on probation or keep him out of confinement in prison. Norm explained that this was strictly up to the judge, and Brutsche added, "Norm had a way with those legislators so that they all walked out of the room perfectly content with what Norm had said."[18]

Judge Gerald Tjoflat related another incident, in which a Congresswoman from New York confronted Norm about the treatment of John Mitchell, the former attorney general who was in a federal facility in Montgomery, Alabama. He had had some kind of surgery, and she claimed that Mitchell had received "Cadillac" treatment. Norm explained to her that they did not do anything different for Mitchell than they did for any other inmate. Judge Tjoflat concluded, "Nobody shoved him around. I can tell you that; he was on top of everything."[19]

Norm's art, and it was an art, of testifying on the hill employed short statements and he never talked too long. He was prepared to answer whatever questions they had and they quickly saw he was an expert on corrections. Furthermore, in terms of budgetary requests, he only asked for what he needed, and they respected him for his honesty and integrity in that regard.

Because of Norm's skill in testifying and making his case before Congress, the Bureau had resources for building new and innovative correctional facilities, for embarking on major training for institutional staff, and for meeting various financial demands necessary for professionalizing the Bureau.

Relationships with the Attorney General's Office and Other Governmental Agencies

Edwin Meese, a former Attorney General, said: "At the time I was the Attorney General, Norm was one of the truly outstanding correctional executives in the country and did an excellent job as the Director of the Bureau of Prisons." Meese went on to say that Norm wanted to retire, but he persuaded him to stay for another year or longer to find a worthy successor.[20]

Chapter 10 - Ripples of Norman Carlson's Leadership

Benjamin Civiletti, another former Attorney General, added,

> I thought Norm worked superbly with the Attorney General's office. The Attorneys General had a lot of respect for Norman, and they would not overstep their role by directing him to do A, B, or C. Rather, they would say, "This is an issue, Norman, what do you think? How would you handle it?" He would say, A, B, or C, and the Attorney General would generally follow his advice.[21]

Civiletti commented on an incident in which he felt that Norm's contributions were extremely helpful to the Attorney General's office. He mentioned the small number of Puerto Rican dissidents who had attacked President Harry Truman and had been in prison for a very long time. They were treated as martyrs in Puerto Rico, and the decision was made to commute their sentences and to release them. Norman Carlson gathered information about the likelihood of their recidivism if released, and with Carlson's assurance that they were good risks for release, their sentences were commuted. Civiletti added that they were never heard from again.

Several associate and assistant attorneys general are quick to agree that Carlson's leadership and credibility with the Attorney General's office and other governmental agencies is what kept politics out of the Bureau of Prisons. Bureau officials also concurred that when Norm was Director, he ran the agency, instead of Congress or the Attorney General's office running the agency. Subsequent to his retirement in 1987, Bureau officials lamented that Congress and the Attorneys General's office had much more control over the agency than they did during the Carlson era.

Rick Seiter, Ph.D., former Bureau of Prisons warden, claimed that the reason the Bureau gained so much respect and esteem in Washington D.C. was because Norm so quickly sized up a political leader.

> He was savvy. He worked with Attorneys Generals who were extremely conservative and those who were extremely

liberal. And he was able to interact and satisfy them both. He was able to see what things were important to them.[22]

Whether it was Congress, Attorneys Generals, deputies, or judges, he worked with, added Seiter, he could see whether the person believed in inmates' rights, cost efficiency, or law and order, and he would package that with good corrections.[23]

Seiter added that Norm was able to give political leaders in each administration enough so that they felt he was responsive to them and to the political mandate they had in terms of the President they served. As a result, they looked upon the Bureau of Prisons as being in good hands. "It is really amazing that he was able to do that."[24]

He concluded by saying that Norm was

> a big builder of coalitions. Every federal judge felt that Norman Carlson walked on water, and most members of Congress felt that he walked on water. I don't think there was anybody of stature in the Department of Justice who worked with Norm that also didn't sing his praise. I have heard him called 'the best manager in federal bureaucracy' and 'the most outstanding leader.' Everyone felt that he was always sensitive to their needs."[25]

The Bureau of Prisons Remained a Career Agency

Another contribution of Carlson's leadership was that the Bureau remained a career agency; apparently, the only agency in the federal government that has remained a career agency, rather than one headed by political appointees from outside the agency.

When Jimmy Carter was elected president in 1976, there was concern that, with a new president, a new director of the Bureau of Prisons might be appointed. At the time, there was the feeling that Ellis C. MacDougall was likely to be appointed Director of the Bureau of Prisons. He had been President Carter's Director of Corrections in Georgia, but he had a health problem and was not appointed as

Director of the Bureau of Prisons. Norman Carlson was kept dangling for months, not knowing if he would be kept on.

Sherman Day, Ph.D., an early director of training for the Bureau, and former director of the National Institute of Corrections, tells in Exhibit 10.3 some of the reasons the President decided to retain Carlson as the Director. This action retained the career agency status of the Bureau.

Exhibit 10.3 There Will Not Be a Change in the Bureau of Prisons

"Now, on the Hill, Norm was magnificent. Let me give you an illustration of how well respected he was. When Jimmy Carter was elected, there was a young man who had worked for the Bureau of Prisons. He left the Bureau to assist in the election of Jimmy Carter and worked very closely with Hamilton Jordan, Jody Powell, and President Carter himself.

"After the election was over, and I know this man very well who reported this conversation to me, Jimmy Carter's people asked him what job he wanted. He said he wanted to be the Director of the Bureau of Prisons. They sent him over to see Griffin Bell, the Attorney General. He sat down with Griffin Bell. Griffin said, 'You have been a very good supporter of the President and have worked very hard. What job are you looking at?' He said, 'I would like to be the Director of the Bureau of Prisons.'

"He told me that Griffin Bell looked at him and said, 'Son, we're not making a change in the Bureau of Prisons. Norman Carlson is over there. I have known him since I was a judge. So, you need to go and consider what else you want, because we're not going to change the Bureau of Prisons.' And I think that is the kind of respect he had built up with judges, Congress, and the Attorney General's office. I think that anyone else would have been out with the change of administration."

Source: Sherman Day, Ph.D., interviewed September 2005.

Federal Witness Protection Programs (WITSEC) Within the Bureau of Prisons

When the Federal Witness Protection Program, or WITSEC, was created in 1970, federal prosecutors were so delighted to have Mafia witnesses testify against other Mafia, or La Cosa Nostra (LCN), family members that they granted them full immunity. Yet, as more and more of the La Cosa Nostra (LCN) agreed to testify, prosecutors and judges became increasingly reluctant to let them go without serving some prison time. By 1974, almost every such criminal who had given testimony against crime leaders had to serve some time before being paroled or relocated. This created a problem: where to house them. The U.S. Marshals Service tried safe houses, military brigs, and country jails, but none of these proved to be satisfactory, primarily because they were deemed unsafe for the witnesses.[26]

Gerald Shur, a career prosecutor with the Criminal Division in the Department of Justice, who is known as the "Father of WITSEC," was the driving force behind creating witness protection in the community. During his thirty-four year tenure, WITSEC protected 6,416 witnesses and 14,468 of their dependents, including wives and children. WITSEC dealt with quite a list of organized criminals, including such notorious organized crime figures as "The Animal" Barboza, Aladena "Jimmy the Weasel" Fratianno, Vincent "Fat Vinnie" Teresa, Henry Hill, Sammy "The Bull" Gravano, and Joseph "Joe Dogs" Iannuzzi. Some 10,000 criminals were convicted because of WITSEC witnesses.[27]

Shur approached Norman Carlson about suitable placement for those in the witness protection program who first had to do prison time, and the Bureau of Prisons' director came up with a solution. He decided to establish a special unit exclusively for government witnesses. The location he had in mind was the third floor of the highrise Metropolitan Corrections Center in New York City. When this jail opened in mid-1978, Shur moved twenty-one government witnesses into the new WITSEC prison unit.[28]

Carlson used a number of security guidelines to keep the third-floor unit separate from the rest of the jail. It had a private security entrance, and every witness in the unit was given an alias to prevent other inmates from knowing his identity. The warden was the only local corrections official who was told the inmate's actual name. Each witness was given a one-person cell, and he was able to ask for his cell door to be locked when other witness were free to play pool or to watch television. Before visitors were permitted to enter the unit, they had to stand in front of a two-way mirror so that the WITSEC witness could verify that the visitor was actually who he claimed to be.

Carlson required every witness to pass an FBI-administered lie detector test before being allowed to be housed in the unit. He wanted to be certain that no one was attempting to sneak into the unit to kill another witness. Even after passing the test, the witness was not automatically admitted into the unit. A photograph of him was passed around to everyone housed there so they could tell correctional officers if they were afraid of the prospective new arrival. Many WITSEC witnesses had grudges against each other and could not be housed together.[29] This program began a close relationship between Carlson and Shur, where Norm initially supported the development of WITSEC units in other federal jails and later on in prison units.

The Metropolitan Correctional Centers in Chicago and San Diego also confined such witnesses on a separate floor. When Shur told Carlson one day, "We need other units to hide prisoners in and we are talking about large numbers," Carlson was not fazed; he simply inquired, "How can we do it?" As WITSEC units were developed in prisons, rather than jails, Carlson continued his strong support (*see* Exhibit 10.4). Indeed, Shur gives credit to Carlson for playing an integral part in developing the Witness Protection Program.[30]

Exhibit 10.4 Norman Carlson's Support for the Witness Protection Program (WITSEC)

"I visited one of the WITSEC units; we had sixty or seventy inmates per unit. The inmates knew that I was coming. They would get together the night before I came and tried to agree what they would complain about tomorrow. I would meet them as a group, and then I would meet with every inmate individually who wished to meet with me. I would spend whatever time it took, twelve hours, whatever. The purpose of the group meeting was to see what the tension level was in the unit. I could feel this extraordinary tension and could see that this thing was about to blow. When I met with the individual inmates, I could see further evidence of this tension. However, I thought it would perhaps dissipate. I had Bureau staff come with me, as well as my own staff, and they were recording the inmates' complaints.

"I got back to Washington the next day. Norm and I were talking on the phone about something else. 'By the way,' Norm asked, 'how did your visit to [such and such an institution] go?' I said, 'Norm, it was the most tense I have ever seen in a unit.' And I went back to this other conversation. Twenty minutes later, the phone rang, and Norm said, 'I just wanted you to know that I have taken care of the problem in [the institution]. I said, 'What do you mean you have taken care of the problem?' He said, 'Oh, I have removed the warden. I transferred him.' He was right; the warden should have been transferred."

Source: Interviewed October 2005.

Norm Carlson was further supportive of the FBI's covert use of prisoners. This occurred when a prisoner would be taken from the Witness Protection Program Unit or from the general prison population, returned to the community for a few days or less to perform a particular mission, and then returned to the prison. When he would get requests from the FBI for the covert use of prisoners, he would ask Shur to filter these requests, because he did not know the agents as well as Shur did. Shur felt that the director was quite open to suggestions and advice related to the covert use of prisoners.[31]

Prison Fellowship Movement

Norm Carlson's acceptance of the Prison Fellowship into the Federal Bureau of Prisons was a leadership decision. Not long after Charles W. Colson was released from a facility of the Bureau of Prisons, he met with Director Carlson in his office. Senator Harold Hughes, who accompanied Colson on this visit, set up the appointment, with these words, "It's about bringing Jesus Christ into prisons."[32]

Colson reported that Senator Hughes was from Iowa, as was Norm Carlson, and they swapped stories about Iowa for a few minutes. Then, Senator Hughes began by asking Carlson if he objected to beginning the meeting with prayer. Carlson indicated that he did not and the senator led the prayer. Senator Hughes continued, "Mr. Carlson, we came here today to tell you of a dream we have for a new work in the federal prisons. We need your cooperation. Chuck will explain."[33]

Colson proceeded by saying that the prison system does not work, and inmates come out worse than when they went in. He contended that "One Person can make a difference—Jesus Christ. His love and power to remake lives is the answer. He will heal and reconcile. I know it. I saw it happen. Give us a chance to prove it."[34]

Colson then asked Norman Carlson if he would issue an order allowing Senator Hughes and himself, or their representatives, to go into any federal prison in the country and select prisoners to bring out for training. Silence prevailed. In his book, *Life Sentence*, Colson reported, "I nearly laughed. It sounded preposterous."[35]

Colson continued in *Life Sentence*, "Carlson's face remained enigmatic, and then he said, 'Let me ask you a question. A few weeks ago my wife and I were at the Terminal Island Prison in Southern California. On Sunday we went to chapel. At one point in the service the chaplain asked the inmates to join in with spontaneous prayers. In the back—I couldn't see him—a man prayed for my wife and me. I was surprised that he did that.'"[36]

Colson went on and said, "I expected Carlson to evade my request, knowing from long experience that no government bureau chief would take such a bold step without consulting his staff, weighing the pros and cons and at least thinking about the impact of his decision on his career. The best I could hope for was that he'd leave the door open just a crack."[37]

"I was stunned, when moments later, Carlson gave us a terse, three-sentence answer. "Go ahead with your plans, Mr. Colson, Senator Hughes. I'll issue the order. Get together with my staff and work out the details."[38]

After the meeting, Norm Carlson issued several executive orders, which opened the way for the first group of prisoners to come to Washington D.C. for two weeks of training. Subsequent to this first training, more than thirty groups have been released, with no major incidents, to receive training so that they could implement prison fellowship groups in their prisons. Exhibit 10.5 contains a letter Mr. Colson sent the author, in which he talks about Norm Carlson's leadership in general and in particular what his leadership has meant to the Prison Fellowship.

Exhibit 10.5 Letter from Charles W. Colson

"So far as I'm concerned, Norman Carlson set the gold standard for leadership in corrections while he was Director of the Bureau of Prisons. I worked with him closely, got to know him very well, and have the absolute highest regard for him. In fact, in the course of my work over the last thirty years, I have met most of the leaders in corrections in America, many of them fine and very dedicated men and women, but no one that I would regard more highly than Norm Carlson.

"I'm sending with this letter a copy of my book *Life Sentence*. In it I describe my relationship with Norm and all that he did in a very innovative way as the Director of the Bureau of Prisons. You can get the story because it was really his permission to us that enabled us to get this ministry off the ground. We're now in 112 countries around the world, a massive prison outreach, running several prisons ourselves.

All of that really became possible because Norm Carlson had the courage, in the face of a lot of resistance, to let us work in his prisons.

"But this was characteristic of Norm Carlson. He was not afraid to challenge the system. He was not afraid to try new things. He showed enormous courage and foresight in the way he handled corrections. He also had a sensible understanding of the problems.

"I know that he developed a close relationship with Chief Justice Warren Burger who also had a keen interest in correctional reform. The Bureau of Prisons was in the vanguard of more enlightened criminal justice policies while Carlson was the director.

"I have a heightened regard for Carlson particularly for his courage. A lot of people get into high government position and then just play on the defense. He was willing to take some chances on some important and significant things to improve the performance of the system and the lives of the men and women confined in it."

Source: Letter received January 20, 2006 and used with permission.

Several high ranking Bureau staff did not approve of this decision. One of the reasons some Bureau staff questioned this decision was that it was a noted break from Bureau of Prisons' procedure because it was not presented to the executive staff as a proposal. It was imposed by Carlson as his approved program and did not contain the collegiality that was the typical way for new programs to be implemented.

The Internship Program

Former Directors Bennett and Alexander used internships. In the 1960s, the Bureau of Prisons had many interns in their offices. During the seventeen years Norman A. Carlson was director, the Bureau of Prisons was quite responsive to college students' internships. One of the most popular internship programs was the one with Kent State University. George Pownall, Ph.D., coordinated it until he retired in 1995. During this time, more than 100 students participated in Bureau of Prisons' internships.

According to Professor Pownall:

> I believe that at least sixty of those who made a career in the Bureau of Prisons started out with an internship. I tried to handpick the student and match him or her with an institution. Some of my students have moved up the ladder. For example, the present Director, Harley Lappin, was one of my interns.[39]

In an interview, Director Lappin told how this internship influenced his choice of career:

> I was a farmer when I went into the Bureau. I went up to Kent State to get my M.A. degree. I met Professor George Pownall, who worked it out that I could do an internship program at the federal institution at Milan [Michigan], and that was my introduction to the Bureau.
>
> Six months later, I came to work as a case manager in Texarkana, Texas. We continue to utilize internships throughout the Bureau today. We have internships for doctorate level psychologists, have an honors program for attorneys, and have general internships.[40]

Another internship that was special with Norm was the one he established with Gustavus Adolphus College in St. Peter, Minnesota. Carlson and his wife had graduated from Gustavus Adolphus College, and the Carlson's' two children had also graduated from the same school. In this program, three interns each semester would be selected. Provided with a paid internship, the student would spend three months in Washington D.C. working in the Director's office and then the next summer in a federal correctional institution.

The fall 2004 *Gustavus Quarterly* reported that seven of the former interns were appointed to positions of great responsibility in the Bureau of Prisons. Paul Laird, former warden of the Federal

Correctional Institution in Coleman, Florida, and the Federal Detention Center in Brooklyn, was recently promoted to assistant director of the Bureau; Lisa Warner Hollingsworth moved from warden of the Correctional Institution in Sandstone, Arizona, to the warden of the Federal Correctional Institution in Cumberland, Maryland; Wendy Roal Warner had been appointed associate warden at the Federal Correctional Institution in Pekin, Illinois; Mark Munson had moved to associate warden at the Federal Correctional Institution in Englewood, Colorado; Richard Engel had been appointed associate warden at the Federal Correctional Institution in Oxford, Wisconsin; Blake Davis had been appointed associate warden at the Federal Medical Center in Rochester, Minnesota; and Teresa Hunt who had been warden of the Federal Correctional Institution in Safford, Arizona recently retired.

The Gustavus internship program lasted from the late 1970s until the late 1980s. In all, about sixty students were involved in this program.

Norm Carlson even invited interns to his home for dinner and for weekends at his cabin in the Blue Ridge Mountains in Virginia. With so much on his plate, the Director still found time to mentor these students. According to some interviewed former interns, Norman Carlson was quite influential in their lives and their careers.

University-Sponsored Research

Norm was instrumental in supporting university-sponsored research when he felt the findings might be of value. David Ward approached Norm and asked "How about doing a study to find out what happened to the inmates who did time at Alcatraz?" Norm, according to Ward, always intellectually curious, agreed. In Exhibit 10.6 Ward tells how his research about two controversial federal prisons—Alcatraz and Marion—was supported.

Exhibit 10.6 University-Sponsored Research

"I was able to get a grant from the National Institute of Justice for the Alcatraz study—I am sure with Norm's support, and from that point on he did everything to assist the project. He assigned one of his research staff to round up inmate and prison files. There is a big difference between a Bureau official calling the record clerk at Leavenworth, for example, and saying, 'Locate all the files of former Alcatraz inmates' than if the call came from some university professor. He paved the way for me to have access to records at the National Archives and got the FBI to send me 'rap sheets' [arrest records] on all 1,550 prisoners.

"Because we got the files so quickly and I found that the inmates were doing so surprisingly well after release, it became clear at the beginning of the project that we had to have information about their post-release experiences. Norm facilitated that part of the study by contacting Don Chamlee at the Administrative Office of U.S. Courts [chief of Federal Probation] to allow my assistants and me access to parole and conditional release records. Mr. Chamlee also arranged for project staff to go to Federal Probation offices across the country to locate parolees including those most difficult to find—men who after release stayed out of prison and were no longer under federal supervision. Their parole officers knew the location of these men and had become quite friendly with them because these high-risk parolees had been successful. Perhaps, the reason for unexpectedly high rate of success is that these particular parolees were intelligent, articulate men who often did not want to talk about doing time on the Rock, even with families or friends, but they felt comfortable discussing these experiences with their parole agents.

"Further into the study when Norm came to a class I was teaching as a visiting professor at the University of California, Berkeley, he commented that the FBI had a new director who wanted to have better interagency cooperation. He suggested that the Bureau of Prisons ask the FBI to allow me access to their files on Alcatraz inmates. Based on this request, I was able to go to the J. Edgar Hoover building in Washington, D.C. and review the records of criminal careers of Alcatraz inmates and FBI investigations of incidents that occurred on the island such as murders and escapes.

"When I discussed interviewing former Alcatraz employees, Norm informed me, 'You can tell every former employee that the Bureau of Prisons will give them a $50 honorarium for taking the time to participate in an interview.' With the Bureau's help, I was able to locate fifty former officers, lieutenants, captains, and wardens. Most of them didn't take the honorarium, but the offer made it clear to them that I had the full support of the Bureau and that they could finally talk about Alcatraz after being prohibited from discussing anything about the prison with outsiders during its thirty years of operation. The Alcatraz study was an example of extraordinary support from a federal agency. Norm, like former Director Bennett, was genuinely interested in the project and both were surprised by the results.

"In 1984, the House Judiciary Committee authorized an investigation of 'conditions' at the federal penitentiary at Marion, Illinois, which had been locked down after two officers were killed during the same day. I don't know how my name came up, but it probably had to do with work I had been doing on Alcatraz for the previous six years. I took on the investigation with Allen Breed and after our report was submitted, I testified before the Judiciary Committee.

"Sometime thereafter I suggested to Norm that it would be worth collecting basic follow-up data on the Marion inmates as I had done in the Alcatraz study. His ready approval provided the basis for the follow up of 1,020 inmates who served time at Marion from the data of the lockdown in October 1983 through the opening of its successor, administrative maximum, at Florence, Colorado. Allowing a university researcher to conduct studies of the federal prison system's most controversial penitentiaries is a measure of Norm's confidence in the management of these prisons and his openness to the findings of research undertaken by investigators independent of the Bureau.

Source: Interviewed March 2008.

In 2009, David Ward published *Alcatraz: The Gangster Years*, the first of two volumes on this famous penitentiary.[41] It is a classic study, by far the best and most interesting study of Alcatraz, and it would not have been possible without the support that Norman Carlson gave to David Ward.

Conclusions

When you consider the totality of Norman Carlson's leadership, it becomes evident that the effects generated from his leadership during the 1970s and 1980s continue today. This is the focus of Chapter 12. What would the witness protection program have been without his locating housing for incarcerated organized criminals in this program? What would the quality of state and local institutional care across the nation be without Carlson's supportive leadership? How detrimental would it have been for the Bureau of Prisons if Carlson had not gained the resources he did because of his credibility with Congress, the Attorney General's office, and other government agencies? The likelihood is that the landscape of corrections, as well as the lives of many touched by these ripples, would be much different if Norman A. Carlson had not been Director of the Bureau of Prisons from 1970 to 1987.

Endnotes

1. Gerald Shur was interviewed October 2005.

2. Tony Travisono was interviewed December 2005.

3. Ibid.

4. Ibid.

5. Ibid.

6. Ibid.

7. NIC

8. Norm Carlson was interviewed July 2006.

9. Bill Wilkey was interviewed November 2005.

10. Dr. Walter Menninger was interviewed October 2005.

11. Information contained on the National Institute of Corrections' Home Page, http://www.nicic.org/Training.

12. Federal Judge Paul Magnuson was interviewed October 2005.

13. Ibid.

14. David C. Jelinek was interviewed December 2005.

15. Peter Bensinger was interviewed October 2005.

16. Wade Houk was interviewed October 2005.

17. Pete Earley said this in an e-mail in November 2005.

18. Dr. Robert Brutsche was interviewed October 2005.

19. Federal Judge Gerald Tjoflat was interviewed December 2005.

20. Former Attorney General Edwin Meese was interviewed October 2005.

21. Benjamin Civiletti was interviewed January 2006.

22. Rick Seiter, Ph.D., was interviewed August 2005.

23. Ibid.

24. Ibid.

25. Ibid.

26. Pete Earley and Gerald Shaw. 2002. *WITSEC: Inside the Federal Witness Protection Program.* New York: Bantam Books, p. 4.

27. Ibid., p. 178.

28. Ibid., p. 179.

29. Shur was interviewed October 2005.

30. Ibid.

31. Ibid.

32. Charles W. Colson. 1979. *Life Sentences.* Tarrytown, NY: Fleming H. Revell Company, p. 44.

33. Ibid., p. 45.

34. Ibid., p. 46.

35. Ibid., p. 47.

36. Ibid.

37. Ibid.

38. Ibid.

39. George Pownall, Ph.D., was interviewed September 2007.

40. Director Harley Lappin was interviewed September 2007.

41. David Ward with Gene Kassebaum. 2009. *Alcatraz: The Gangster Years.* Berkeley: University of California Press.

Chapter 11

From a Good to a Great Organization

Good is the enemy of great. And that is one of the key reasons why we have so little that becomes great. We don't have great schools, principally because we have good schools. We don't have great government, principally because we have good government. Few people attain great lives, in large part because it is just so easy to settle for a good life. The vast majority of companies never become great because the vast majority become quite good—and that is their main problem.

Jim Collins[1]

An examination reveals the many ways that the Federal Bureau of Prisons or any correctional system, or for that matter any prison, falls short of being "great." These shortcomings of prisons or correctional systems can be placed in the following categories: (1) high recidivism rates; (2) negative institutional impact; (3) bad things happen in prisons that certainly affect the quality of life for both inmates and staff; (4) courts document the failure of prisons for frequently neglecting to provide for the constitutional rights of inmates; and (5) international comparisons of U.S. prisons to the best in other countries reveal that U.S. prisons compare poorly with prisons in some other countries. We will examine each of these shortcomings.

High Recidivism Rates

Every study shows that adult correctional institutions have high recidivism rates. More than 60 percent of released subjects followed for five years or more fail; in other words, they commit a new criminal act or are violated for failure to comply with parole or conditions of their release. This failure rate has been consistent through the years and seems to be independent of any program or intervention in which prisoners have been involved. Interestingly, one of the few studies that found low recidivism rates for institutional release was done by David Ward on parolees who had done time in Alcatraz 1934-1963.[2]

Some argue that inmates have little or no employment history, a history of drug and alcohol abuse, and a pattern of repeated failures in nearly everything they have done; therefore, we might expect that this population would have difficulty in community adjustment. This may explain why they are returned time after time to institutional settings. Nevertheless, the fact still remain that one of the basic purposes of prisons—to reduce recidivism when inmates return to the streets—is not successful.

Institutional Impact

One of the most serious criticisms of correctional institutions is that they are harmful to inmates. Walter Reckless and his students spent the decade of the 1960s in Ohio examining the institutional impact of juvenile and adult correctional institutions and failed to find any measureable positive impact of institutionalization.[3] Bartollas, Miller, and Dinitz, in an examination of an end-of-the-line juvenile facility in Ohio, in the early 1970s concluded:

> This is certainly not the first, nor is it likely to be the last, in a long series of books, monographs, and articles which indict the juvenile correctional system as anti-therapeutic, anti-rehabilitative, and as exploitative and demeaning of keepers and kept alike. The juvenile correctional institutions,

not unlike every other type of total institution, is or can be far more cruel and inhumane than most outsiders ever imagine. The dynamics of a large juvenile correctional institution is not the inverse of the real, the outside, world. In that both indigenous and imported patterns combine, the juvenile institution is a culmination of the worst features of a free society. . . .

If this research has taught us anything, it is the wisdom contained in two disparate but appropriate and slightly modified quotations:

Man is a wolf to man.

No pain equals an injury inflicted under pretense of justice punishment (or rehabilitation).[4]

Michael Massoglia, Ph.D., tells how his study of institutionalization revealed that incarceration has a negative impact on the physical health of African Americans, and that their disproportionate confinement rates are a major contributing factor in their later health problems in the community, including increased numbers with infectious diseases, TB, and hepatitis. At the same time, he found that incarceration is more stressful to whites than African Americans and that it represents more of a stigma to whites than African Americans when they are released from prison.[5]

Quality of Life: Bad Things Happen in Prison

We identified the necessary relationship between quality of life and a humane prison in Chapter 8. We noted that Norm Carlson attempted to incorporate these ingredients of quality into the Bureau of Prisons. For example, his intent was to treat inmates with decency and respect, to keep them safe, and to protect staff. Clearly, as this biography documents, this did not always happen. There was a fire in which inmates lost their lives, inmates assaulted and murdered each other, and staff lost their lives at the U.S. Penitentiary Marion and in other Bureau of Prisons' facilities over the years.

When you turn to the various inmate memoirs written from prison, as well as investigative reports on prisons, you anticipate that you will get a healthy dose of the inmate saying how he has been mistreated, and you are not disappointed. Michael G. Santos, one of the articulate voices from prison—and he has done all his time in federal prisons—had this to say about incarceration:

> From the director to the prison guard, the mantra has become to *preserve the security of the institution.* That translates into governing by policy rather than by common sense, to implementing and enforcing a rigid culture of us versus them that stymies individual growth. Rather than encouraging the growth of citizens, the prison system has become a thoughtless beast that many unthinkingly and unquestionably fight to preserve.
>
> Men locked inside of cages resist the machine's efforts to weaken them. In their efforts to establish some kind of identity, many prisoners continue the cycle of behavior that brought them to prison in the first place. In response, the machine applies more pressure, creating greater hostility and distancing offenders further from the values of society. The cycle never ends. Like Viking [an inmate Santos knew], many prisoners leave prison even less prepared to function in society than when they began serving their terms. Taxpayers receive an unbelievably poor return on the incredible investment they have made to fund the American prison system.[6]

Federal Court Intervention

From the time that Norm Carlson began as director in 1970 to his retirement in 1987, the courts, especially federal courts, found it necessary to involve themselves in prisons. In some correctional systems, namely Arkansas, Alabama, and Texas, long and expensive court action required a nearly total overhaul of the system. Many charges of brutality and sometimes outright corruption were alleged. However, even in the most progressive systems, with professional administration, inmates were constantly bringing cases before the courts. Indeed, by the time that Carlson retired in 1987, thirty-seven correctional departments were operating under court order.

The good news is that in progressive systems, with enlightened administrators and well-trained staff, the vast majority of inmate cases was dismissed or inmates gained no relief. The bad news is that judicial intervention was necessary to raise the constitutional rights that inmates received. At times, inmates were treated in scandalous ways, and court intervention was necessary to correct this.

U.S. Prisons Compared to Other Prisons

Prisons are not generally looked to as model and humane facilities. Alvin J. Bronstein, former director of the American Civil Liberties Union Prison Project, defined a humane prison:

> There aren't any. The definition in my dictionary of humane is having the best quality of human beings, kind, tender, merciful, sympathetic, civilizing, and humanizing. There are no prisons in the world that have those qualities. I have visited marvelous prisons, one in particular in Denmark.
>
> In fact, the warden or governor of that prison [was] the late Eric Anderson. His prison in Ringe, Denmark has been written up in many national and international publications and was the subject of a program on *Sixty Minutes*. It was one of the most interesting and thoughtful and decent prisons I have ever been to. I have visited it about six times because Anderson was a friend. Each time I would leave the prison I would say, "Eric, this is just a marvelous institution you're running." He would always say, "Yes, Al, but remember all

prisons damage people and this prison, as good as it is, may also damage people."

This answer to this question is that when you look at a prison, it must be inhumane because it is totally different from being in a free society. You are not free to make decisions about most things that go on in the day. When you get up, what you eat, and what you're going to do, those decisions are made for you. Accordingly, it is a dehumanizing experience, but that can be minimized My idea of a good prison is one that does not make persons worse when they leave than when they came in, that doesn't make them less able to function in the real world and most prisons do that.[7]

In sum, the conclusion of this section is that prison systems, even the Federal Bureau of Prisons—long a standard-setting system—cannot be considered great. Prison work is tough work. Prisons are often violent places, and frequently only the strong survive in these settings.

A Correctional Expert Evaluates the Bureau of Prisons

Norman Carlson had gotten to know John DiIulio, a well-known professor who writes about corrections, through his mentor, Professor James Q. Wilson at Harvard, and had read DiIulio's book on state prison management and invited him to take a look at the Bureau of Prisons' operations. DiIulio accepted his invitation and visited the Federal Correctional Institution (FCI) in Butner, North Carolina.[8] He was so impressed that he began a study of the Bureau of Prisons. Exhibit 11.1 contains his comments about the quality of what went on in the Bureau of Prisons' facilities.

Exhibit 1.1 Quality of What Went on in the Bureau of Prisons' Facilities

"Carlson articulated the BOP's historic mission as operating prisons in which inmates enjoyed 'safety, humanity, and opportunity.' He saw no contradiction between strict administrative controls and tight discipline on the one hand, and the provision of basic amenities (such as good food and clean cells) and life-enhancing programs (from remedial reading to vocational training).

"FCI Butner put these ideas into practice. Inmates chose programs as they wished. Restrictions on inmate movement were minimal. By the time I visited the prison, it had a decade's worth of statistics and studies behind it. In sum, they showed that it had done nothing to reduce recidivism (or, for that matter, to improve prisoners' post-release ability to get and keep jobs). But the studies also hinted at reduced violence, increased rates of inmate participation in (and completion of) educational and other programs, and lowered staff turnover and job-related stress.

"The quality of life inside Butner was amazing compared to what one could see in most state medium and high security prisons. When I visited Butner its warden was Sam Samples, an agency veteran with a doctorate in education, who followed the principle of 'management by walking around.' The prison staff was on top of things. Every unit sparkled. The food was excellent. The work areas hummed. No shouting. No aggressive horseplay. Little inmate idleness. In short, there were few of the unpleasant sights and sounds I had come to expect when observing life behind bars."

Source: John J. DiIulio, Jr., 1990. "Prisons That Work: Management is the Key." *Federal Prison Journal,* Summer, pp. 7-14.

DiIulio's analysis concluded that it was sound management that brought about the safe and humane conditions of the Bureau of Prisons. It can be argued that Butner did not have high security and violent inmates, and it is questionable whether you can extend what took place at Butner to more security-oriented penitentiaries. Carlson, according to DiIulio, realized when he became director in the early 1970s that it was imperative for the agency to carry out its mission in the most professional manner possible.

DiIulio continued:

> Over time, the BOP had instituted a number of practices designed to ensure 'field compliance' with Washington's policy directives: frequent transfer of personnel from prison to prison, an elaborate system of internal audits (fiscal and operational), and a common training program for all employees. Each institution would have its special operational needs, and Washington would make provisions for those.[9]

One secret of the Bureau of Prisons' success, DiIulio noted, was that "all institutions operated on the same principles via the same basic procedures." Individuals who came to the Bureau with "experience in other prison systems were screened carefully and retrained extensively."[10] Carlson made the decision to restructure the agency into five regions, each with its own headquarters and regional director. This was Carlson's way of reinforcing accountability and control. Unit management was emphasized throughout the Bureau. Teams of security staff and counselors were placed in charge of a given wing or 'unit.' This raised the quality of life within the unit, as the unit was responsible for everything from sanitation to keeping track of prisoners' activities and release dates.[11]

In addition, Carlson sponsored seminars, meetings, and award ceremonies because of his concern to deepen the 'family' culture of the Bureau of Prisons. The frequent moves among staff, which encouraged them to anchor their social lives with other agency workers and their families, also contributed to developing this family culture.

DiIulio goes on: "The talk of the agency as family is more than a metaphor: 'Bureau brat'—children or grandchildren of agency workers—can be found in most Federal prisons. The current warden of USP Lewisburg has a father, two brothers, and a son, all of whom worked in the BOP."[12]

DiIulio concluded that there were also other reasons why the management of the Bureau of Prisons was outstanding:

- The Bureau of Prisons had a continuity of good leadership in the past
- Carlson kept abreast of legal changes, striving always to stay one step ahead of the courts
- The agency was committed to excellence
- Wardens kept in contact with what was going on with staff and inmates on a regular basis
- The Bureau of Prisons maintained the cleanliness of its prisons
- The Bureau of Prisons had a uniform disciplinary process

Conclusions

This chapter noted that "greatness" found in the organizational literature, especially in evaluating profit-making companies, cannot be applied to punishment-oriented organizations. Prisons, even the very best of them, have too many reasons to detract from their being "great" institutions. Nevertheless, the Federal Bureau of Prisons has long set the standards for American corrections, and under the able leadership of Norm Carlson became better.

John DiIulio, Jr., known to be a sharp critic of correctional systems, examined the Bureau of Prisons and lavished extensive praise on this agency. He began his assessment impressed with the Butner facility, and his admiration for this federal correctional system continued to grow. He, at the end, like this present author, concluded that Norman A. Carlson was an outstanding leader and that the Federal Bureau of Prisons is an excellent prison system.

Endnotes

1. Jim Collins. 2001. *Good to Great.* New York: *Harper Business*, p. 1.

2. See David Ward and Gene Kassebaum. 2009. *Alcatraz: The Gangster Years.* Berkeley California: University of California Press.

3. Walter C. Reckless. 1967. *The Crime Problem, 4th Ed.* New York: Appleton-Century-Crofts.

4. Clemens Bartollas, Stuart J. Miller, and Simon Dinitz. 1976. *Juvenile Victimization: The Institutional Paradox.* New York: Halsted Press, pp. 259, 273.

5. Bartollas interviewed Michael Massoglia, Ph.D., in March 2007. See also Michael Massoglia, 2008. "Incarceration as Exposure: The Prison Infectious Disease and Other Stress-Related Illnesses," in *Journal of Health and Social Behavior 49*: 1, 56-71.

6. Michael G. Santos. 2006. *Inside: Life Behind Bars in America.* New York: St. Martin's Press, pp. 281-282.

7. Interviewed and quoted in Clemens Bartollas. 2004. *Becoming a Model Warden: Striving for Excellence.* Alexandria, Virginia: American Correctional Association, p. 150.

8. John J. DiIulio, Jr. 1990. "Prisons That Work: Management is the Key." *Federal Prison Journal,* Summer. p. 7-14.

9. Ibid.

10. Ibid.

11. Ibid.

12. Ibid.

13. Ibid. and John D. DiIulio, Jr. 1994. "Principled Agents: The Cultural Bases of Behavior in a Federal Government Bureaucracy," *Journal of Public Administration Research and Theory 4*, pp. 277-318.

Part III — Norman Carlson's Contributions to the Present Correctional Community

Chapter 12

Norman Carlson's Influence on Corrections

Norm possessed an incredible array of characteristics which made him an exceptional leader. First and foremost, Norm's strength of character and his integrity were unquestioned. No one could be more honest, candid, and direct in their role as leader. His vast knowledge of the field of corrections and his clear picture of where the Bureau of Prisons fit in the federal criminal justice arena, enabled him to approach all situations with a "big picture" view that caused the rest of us to marvel at his ability. He communicated his direction and expectations with such clarity that there was little doubt as to what was to be done. His commitment to ensuring the Bureau of Prisons remained a policy driven organization was critical in ensuring a consistent, cohesive agency as the Bureau of Prisons grew so dramatically over the years.

Kathleen Hawk Sawyer, Ed.D.[1]

This statement by Kathleen Hawk Sawyer, former Director of the Federal Bureau of Prisons, shows the respect that Norm has in the Bureau of Prisons. She also noted that Norm's commitment to the Bureau of Prisons and its staff was evident in how well he represented the Bureau of Prisons before the Department of

Justice, the federal judiciary, and Congress. She asserted that the Bureau of Prisons is "the effective and respected organization that it is today due to the leadership of Norm Carlson." He "taught an entire generation of Bureau of Prisons' staff how to run an effective corrections agency. His ability to adapt to changing times enabled him to keep the Bureau of Prisons current and relevant."[2]

Present Bureau of Prisons Director, Harley Lappin, in the Introduction to this book, addressed the lasting impact that Norman Carlson had on the Bureau of Prisons. In Exhibit 12.1, Director Lappin, describes the influence that Norman Carlson has had on the Bureau of Prisons:

Exhibit 12.1 Influence of Norman Carlson on the Bureau of Prisons

"Norman Carlson still has huge influence on the Bureau of Prisons today. He, in my opinion, has exceptional leadership skills, which were expressed by the changes that took place in the Bureau of Prisons while he was director. He has [communicated] and continues to effectively communicate his message about correctional issues to staff at all levels of the agency, as well as [to] individuals outside the agency with great vision and foresight into issues that impact the field of corrections. Norm was very persuasive and always able to influence the attitudes and opinions of others who have an interest in advancing the corrections profession.

"I know he took great interest in and led during his time as Director a number of programs and changes that are still found in the Bureau:

- He professionalized staff training.
- He implemented our inmate classification system.
- He oversaw the implementation of SENTRY, which is the Bureau's primary automated inmate management system. [SENTRY provides immediate access to the current institutional population; it further calculates all aspects of inmates'

sentences and is the means by which inmates are assigned to specific facilities].
- Norm also fostered the unit management concept into a standard operation.
- He also promoted the direct supervision of inmates and established a constructive communication with inmates as a sound correctional practice that should be adhered to by all corrections workers.
- He fully implemented community corrections in the Bureau of Prisons.

"Those were a few of the things that Norm contributed to the agency that are still with us today. When I became director, Kathy talked about what Mike Quinlan [preceding director] had shared with her. As I talked with Mike, what was interesting was the consistency of what was important and the vision we had for the Bureau. We all did not necessarily agree on how to accomplish that, but similar direction has carried over from Norm, to Mike, to Kathy, and to me. There has been consistency on the values of the Bureau of Prisons and the mission.

"We do things a little differently than they did, but the core principles are adhered to, and this led to less confusion among our staff even though leadership was transitioning to different people."

Source: Interviewed in 2007.

Carlson's influence is still part of the Bureau of Prisons. He changed the agency's approach to inmate management, as he de-emphasized the Medical Model and implemented the "Balanced Model" of corrections. He directed the Bureau's expansion, including the creation of a new type of administrative prison facility located in major metropolitan areas. These Metropolitan Correctional Centers were designed to hold inmates of all security levels.

He also implemented regionalization of the agency (in other words, splitting the Bureau into regions with oversight provided by a regional director and regional staff). This enhanced oversight of the increasing number of institutions and inmates, thereby improving the effectiveness of institution management. He established the Bureau's executive staff. Its membership included division assistant directors and regional directors, who were, in turn, responsible for specific areas of oversight and provided the Director their subject-matter expertise to guide the agency into the future.

In addition, he expanded protection of inmate rights by implementing an inmate grievance process. He emphasized and promoted a proactive approach to dealing with legal rulings, keeping bureau policy consistent with legal rulings and even ahead of the cure in terms of planning for integrating legal decisions related to corrections. He also directed the agency's management of and response to the influx of Mariel Cuban inmates/detainees and related issues.[3]

While Norm was busy implementing reforms at the Bureau of Prisons, other courageous leaders were toiling in state and local corrections. Often, due to the influence of what was happening in the federal system, they were able to make changes in their state system. Perhaps part of the changes that occurred among states were due to the model that Norm Carlson was setting. Other changes occurred due to the leadership of some excellent people, often friends of Carlson.

State Corrections and the Emergence from the Dark Ages

Ellis C. MacDougall, former director of five correctional departments in the United States, professor of criminal justice at the University of South Carolina, and ACA President (1969), argues that significant positive changes took place in corrections in the 1960s and 1970s:

> You first have to realize where corrections has come. It's only in the last few years that corrections has come out of the Dark Ages. We still have a lot of problems in corrections, but we have come a long way. Let me illustrate by my experience.

When I became commissioner of the South Carolina Department of Corrections in 1962, we fed inmates on twenty-nine cents a day. There was open gambling on the yard. We weren't able to turn the system around until we started to get federal help in the late 1960s. Then, we were able to develop training programs and hire qualified staff.

In 1968 when I became commissioner of corrections in Connecticut, the jails—which were built in 1830—still had buckets in the cells. It is now a very good system. In 1971 when I went to Georgia as director, the deputy director of that major system had been a political appointee. He was a former disc jockey and a car salesman. Political patronage had reduced that system to a shambles.

When I went to Mississippi in the early 19070s to become director, they did not have a Department of Corrections. I was asked to set up the legislation to establish a department and to stay and get it organized. At Parchment, the Mississippi State Prison was a plantation with some nineteen camps scattered over 10,000 acres. The buildings were ramshackle, and most of the inmates worked on the vast farm. The place was rampant with disorder. The inmates ran the system.

In 1978, when I was asked by then Governor George Babbit to take over the Arizona Department of Corrections, they had had five directors in a year. At the Arizona State Prison, they had three gangs, the Black Guerrilla Army, the Mexican Mafia, and the Aryan Brotherhood, and they were at war. They were having a stabbing a week and killing a month. With management changes and introduction of meaningful programs, we had one stabbing the first year and then four years without another serious assault.

> I felt that after completing the changes made in these five states, we had turned the corner and corrections was moving toward reform. My goal was a system that would incarcerate the hard-core inmate humanely but offer opportunity to the balance of the population to complete their education or learn a marketable skill followed by a release program that would assimilate them back into society.

Former Director MacDougall made several important assertions. First, state corrections has emerged from the Dark Ages. To indicate how true his perspective was, corrections observers look to the so-called Dark Ages of Corrections. During this period, discipline in American prisons was rough and physical, and public flogging was not unusual. Until 1966 when the federal courts outlawed the practice, prisoners in Mississippi and Arkansas were punished with the strap. Prison work traditionally was miserable and punitive. Pay, if any, was in pennies. Some states had coal mines in which prisoners were required to labor regardless of their skill or experience in mining. The danger of working in such conditions was great, but concern for the safety of convicts was not a priority.

Having made their case about the brutality of the past, corrections observers then point with pride to progressive changes in corrections. Gone are breaking on the wheel; public hanging; disemboweling, and quartering; flogging; the sweatbox; the lockstep; and convicts in striped suits splitting blocks of stone with sledgehammers. In addition, the quality and services of institutional food have improved. Vocational and educational programs have expanded and improved in most institutions. These include programs in computer use, horticulture, fish hatchery management, barbering and cosmetology, welding, machine shop work, electronics, baking, plumbing, automobile body and fender repair, and many others.

Some inmates are employed by free-world enterprises that pay them wages of near free-world levels. Minimum- and medium-security prisons provide humane alternatives to life confinement. And perhaps most significantly, the standards and accreditation process of the American Correctional Association has been implemented in increasing numbers of juvenile and adult correctional agencies throughout the United States.

Second, Director MacDougall asserted that strong leadership has been vitally important in the reform that has taken place in state corrections. "Too often we design and organize our systems to fail. I attribute all the changes I've been able to make to management. We need to deliver a product effectively and to go after quality personnel. Professional management can do much for corrections."[5]

Richard A. McGee, for example, changed the nature of corrections in California by upgrading the physical plants and staffing patterns, for instituting research, and by developing alternatives to imprisonment. Kenneth Stoneman closed Vermont's only maximum-security prison in the 1970s. Lloyd McCorkle, instead of building more prisons, developed a network of satellites at other human service institutions. Kenneth F. Schoen was instrumental in laying out the principles of Minnesota's groundbreaking Community Corrections Act. James V. Bennett closed Alcatraz, opened Marion, planned Morgantown, and created a professional bureaucracy at the Federal Bureau of Prisons. Elayn Hunt led Louisiana corrections out of its dark ages.

In the 1980s and 1990s, exemplary state directors/commissioners and state wardens moved corrections forward. They included the following. Frank Wood, Minnesota's commissioner and warden, played a valued role in bringing reform to the Minnesota Department of Corrections. Chase Riveland, former commissioner of corrections in Washington State, brought reform to his state and served as an important voice in national corrections for more than three decades. Reginald Wilkinson, Ed.D., director of the Ohio Department of Rehabilitation and Corrections, focused on improving the quality of institutional life. Mary Leftridge Byrd, former superintendent of several facilities, and Jim Bruton, former Minnesota warden, are further examples of excellent leadership in state corrections. Their efforts helped move corrections forward.

MacDougall also suggested that the Federal Bureau of Prisons had been helpful in his process of penal reform. The Bureau of Prisons, as state administrators are quick to discover, has been helpful to state departments of corrections in their receptivity toward transferring some of the most intractable inmates from states, in the counsel the Bureau of Prisons has been quick to provide to states, in the financial resources states sometimes received from federal agencies, and in the example the Bureau of Prisons provided of how it is possible to operate correctional institutions humanely and effectively.

Influence of Norman Carlson on Contemporary State Corrections

In addition to the effect that Carlson's leadership continues to have on the Federal Bureau of Prisons, he was also influential with state departments of corrections. Director Carlson had a number of factors on his side in terms of affecting state agencies. He was director for a long period, seventeen years; he had great visibility, constantly receiving nationwide newspaper coverage; he was president of the American Correctional Association; and he was widely respected by nearly everyone who met him. Carlson's main areas of contributions to state departments included modeling the use of professional management techniques for correctional administrators; professionalization of institutional staff; proactive leadership; adoption of standards and accreditation; and the avoidance of corruption.

Professional Management of Correctional Administrators

Carlson influenced state and private corrections in terms of professional management in a number of ways. First, he emphasized the importance of educational credentials and institutional background in terms of qualifications for directors/commissioners and superintendents/wardens. It was not unusual for directors and wardens in state, local, and private corrections to be political appointees and to have no correctional experience when Carlson became director of the Bureau of Prisons in 1970s. However, by the 1990s and early years of the twenty-first century, this took place much less frequently in state, local, and private corrections. We can attribute this change in part due to the example of professional management Carlson and other Bureau of Prisons administrators and managers displayed.

Second, another emphasis of Carlson was his focus on clarity of mission of the Federal Bureau of Prisons. (The current mission statement is in the Foreword to this book). In 1970, from the very beginning of his administration, Norman Carlson wanted the Bureau of Prisons to have a clear mission. In the mission statement adopted during Carlson's administration, the basic approach was a balanced one. Public safety was paramount, but, at the same time, inmates' rights were ensured. Inmates were given opportunities to change and improve themselves. Administrators began to view reducing recidivism as an important goal of corrections.

When Carlson became director, only Connecticut, Minnesota, and Texas did not have the drift of confusion, which had been a debilitating problem for many correctional systems. Today, increasingly numbers of local, state, and private systems are seeking to develop a meaningful mission statement—which often is defined as the realization of a safe and humane system.

Third, Carlson strongly supported the idea that wardens need to manage by walking around (MBWA) the prison. He did not believe that it was possible to effectively manage a prison by staying in your office or out of touch with inmates

Carlson wanted his wardens to have a hands-on approach to prison administration. Carlson felt that this was the only way to know what actually was going on in institutions. Some state wardens in the past, such as Joseph Ragen and a host of recent wardens, support the importance of walking around the institution. The fact that this practice was so widespread in federal prisons seems to have had some influence on state and private prisons. State wardens found out about it because they talked with federal wardens at conventions and conferences.

Fourth, Carlson advocated that prisons should be headed by a professional administrator who was both knowledgeable and alert. Carlson knew what was going on in the field, in both national and international correctional systems. He believed that you needed to keep up with what was going on in the world and that you could not isolate yourself. He wanted to hear the viewpoints of those he considered knowledgeable about particular issues. For example, Carlson consulted with such widely respected experts as law professors, Norval Morris and James Jacobs; political scientist, John Dilulio, Jr.; psychiatrist, Dr. Walter Menninger; and law expert, Alvin Bronstein. The image of the informed administrator generated by his seventeen years of leadership in the Bureau of Prisons provided a model that others in state, private, and local corrections soon emulated.

Fifth, the emphasis he placed on accountability, attention to detail, and firm compliance with schedules and inmate movement resulted in staff having greater control of their facility and in inmates knowing what to expect from prison operations. State wardens also began to emphasize accountability, detail, and compliance with schedules and inmate movements more than they had in the past. It is reasonable to believe that the usually better managed federal facilities influenced state and private administrators to examine why this was so and to realize that such matters as accountability, detail, schedules, and inmate movements were absolute necessities for inmate control. These emphases of the Bureau of Prisons were communicated to state corrections administrators at American Correctional Association meetings, in publications and documents, and when federal agencies hosted training at the National Institute of Corrections for state administrators.

Professionalization of Staff

Norm's vision of corrections as a profession was one of the earliest themes he articulated once he became director of the Bureau of Prisons. Director Bennett had previously focused on professionalization in the Federal Bureau of Prisons, and some states' departments of corrections, such as Connecticut, Minnesota, and California, saw professionalization as a major part of their corrections mission.

The signs of professionalism currently impact state, country, and private corrections. They are taught in state correctional training academies across the nation. They receive focus in the programs of accreditation and certification of professionals of the American Correctional Association. The spirit of professionalism has contributed to the emphasis on integrity, to the treatment of inmates, to the avoidance of unethical behaviors, and to the commitment to create a workplace that is safe, healthy, and free of harassment. Some states' correctional agencies moved more quickly than others, but this spirit of professionalism is now generally found throughout the nation.

Standards and Accreditation: The American Correctional Association

Perhaps Norman Carlson's biggest contribution to American corrections is the role he played in the development of the accreditation standards of the American Correctional Association. As previously suggested, Griffin Bell, the Attorney General, wanted to have federal standards developed, and it was primarily because of Norman Carlson's intervention that Bell and the following Attorney General, Benjamin Civiletti, agreed to drop the possibility of federal standards, which thereby made it possible for the American Correctional Association to develop its standards that have been so well received in corrections. In 2009, 1,280 correctional services across the United States were ACA accredited, including the following:

- 6 adult correctional boot camp programs
- 18 correctional agencies' administration
- 613 adult correctional institutions
- 252 adult community residential facilities
- 3 adult day reporting programs
- 120 adult local detention facilities
- 3 adult probation and parole authorities
- 18 adult probation and parole field services
- 9 correctional industries
- 1 small jail
- 18 correctional academies
- 6 electronic monitoring programs

- 1 food services program
- 11 health care programs
- 9 therapeutic communities
- 5 juvenile correctional boot camp programs
- 57 juvenile correctional facilities (formally training schools)
- 66 juvenile community residential facilities
- 37 juvenile detention facilities
- 21 juvenile day treatment programs
- 12 juvenile probation and aftercare services
- 2 small juvenile detention facilities

Proactive Leadership

Norm was proactive before the term became popular. He believed it was important to get ahead of the curve. He saw more emerging trends and issues that should be addressed early. He did not believe in permitting problems to simmer longer than necessary. Yet, he was good at distinguishing those issues that were ephemeral and not acting precipitously. He wanted to be anticipatory and preventative so that institutional problems, as much as possible, could be avoided.

Significantly, an increasing number of proactive wardens and heads of corrections systems began to appear in correctional leadership across the nation. Even with the political agenda in some states and the financial restrictions in most states, which have brought repressive measures to correctional facilities, the leadership of these proactive correctional administrations is one of the most encouraging signs of corrections early in the twenty-first century.

Avoidance of Corruption

Norm Carlson placed great emphasis on integrity in the operation of correctional institutions. His emphasis on integrity led to the development of an Office of Internal Affairs. Carlson wanted to avoid corruption and abuses within the Bureau of Prisons. The Bureau of Prisons still had problems with corruption. In the California, Federal Correctional Institution at Terminal Island, California, as previously suggested, fifty-one staff members were accused of various forms of corruption.

Nevertheless, Carlson and the Bureau emphasized integrity and corruption-free correctional operations. This provided a standard for state agencies, so many of which had their own problems with various forms of corruption. All the evidence points to the conclusion that the end result of this emphasis on integrity is that the forms of corruption have been reduced in state agencies, and the examples of corruptions that arise are the exceptions rather than what takes place on a regular basis.

Conclusions

This brief chapter has considered an important question: What is Norman A. Carlson's influence on corrections more than twenty years following his retirement from the Bureau of Prisons? Director Harley Lappin, present Director of the Federal Bureau of Prisons addresses some of the influence he feels that Carlson has had on the Bureau of Prisons. The remainder of the chapter then considers contributions that Carlson appears to continue to have on state corrections. It is clear that corrections is facing some serious problems today, but it would be much shortchanged without the formative influence of the Director of the Bureau of Prisons, Norman A. Carlson.

Endnotes

1. Former Director, Kathleen Hawk Sawyer, was interviewed September 2005.

2. Ibid.

3. Page sent by the Archives Office of the Bureau of Prisons, entitled "Norm Carlson's Accomplishments with Long-Term Impact on the Agency." This is undated and has not been published.

4. Interviewed January 1979 and November 2000.

5. Interviewed April 1979.

Chapter 13

Norman Carlson's Other Contributions to Corrections

Peter Bensinger, former director of the Drug Enforcement Administration (DEA) and the Illinois Department of Corrections, as well as a former Assistant Attorney General, made this evaluative statement about Norman Carlson:

> What I saw in Norm is someone who inspired loyalty and enthusiasm with people who worked in a difficult and not often appreciated assignment. With Norm as their leader, corrections had a sense that they had a leader who believed in their mission and in those who worked for the Bureau of Prisons. He was really effective in dealing with Congress, the public, and cabinet interests by not letting politics interfere with what needed to be done in an individual institution. In a situation like a federal agency that has fifty or more facilities spread all over the country, you have all kinds of pressure on how to employ people, but Norm was able to make it all work. He was able to put programs and facilities where they needed to be, not just where some appropriation committee representative would want the facility.[1]

When you examine all of Norman Carlson's contributions, it is clear that he contributed a paradigm shift to corrections. Without Carlson's leadership in the 1970s and 1980s, corrections would clearly be a much different field today.

This chapter proposes a different avenue of inquiry. It examines a number of Carlson's beliefs and ideas that were part of his leadership, that are not yet fully implemented—especially in state corrections. They include the following:

- He believed that corrections is not a partisan issue.
- He strongly believed that the dichotomy between custody and treatment must be eliminated.
- He supported the building of prisons that in both form and function expressed his correctional philosophy.
- He recognized and supported the development of leadership.

Corrections is Not a Partisan Issue

Norman Carlson has always strongly believed that corrections is not a partisan issue. Yet, the history of state and county corrections shows that corrections has been very much a partisan issue. This means that with every change of political office, a new top corrections administrator is likely to be appointed. When corrections is so interwoven with the political process, individuals can be appointed to correctional leadership, who may be friends with the governor or the sheriff in county corrections, but have no background in and limited skills for correctional leadership. It is less true today than in the past, but too many horrible stories still exist—top correctional appointments were totally unprepared for their new position and the results were not surprising.

Furthermore, because their jobs are very political, corrections directors tend to ride the fence and to maintain the status quo. They know what appears to be a success one day is often considered a failure the next. Gordon H. Faulkner, former director of corrections in Indiana, expressed it this way, "Corrections is swept along today. Correctional professionals don't set directions. We are appointed and have no job security. As a result, we have a tendency to do what we are told."[2]

The present author experienced the instability of correctional leadership when he interviewed thirty-five of the heads of state correctional systems and the director of the Federal Bureau of Prisons in

1979. By 1982, three years later, only a handful of these leaders, including Director Carlson, still had their jobs. Carlson worked very hard to professionalize the Federal Bureau of Prisons. He wanted the Executive Department to view the Bureau of Prisons as a career agency, and he was able to achieve this goal.

One major advantage of the continuity of leadership is the ability to develop staff, to to fully use their talents and possibilities. At times, corrections needs a new start and reorganization is required. Prisons may be out of control, placing both inmates and staff in dangerous environments. In such situations, staff is demoralized and new leadership must be appointed. Still, on the whole, the more stable the leadership, the more likely that staff engagement and the integrity of programs will be enhanced.

The Dichotomy Between Custody and Treatment Must Be Eliminated

Traditionally, the world of corrections is divided into two worlds: custody and treatment. As a new employee in corrections discovers the first day on the job, custody is the absolute priority in a correctional facility. Unless a correctional facility is secure, nothing else takes place. This frequently means that treatment staff are relegated to a minor place or position and are informed explicitly and implicitly that they are minor players in what takes place in a correctional facility. Inmates, of course, are cognizant of the minor role of treatment agents within the facility. Unfortunately, sometimes open conflict exists between security and treatment staff.

Norman Carlson, in contrast, attempted to eliminate the dichotomy between custody and treatment by uniting the two, especially at the unit level, into one role. The correctional officer in the unit is responsible for both custody and treatment. This concept was reinforced in the Federal Bureau of Prisons' staff training centers where all new employees, regardless of position, went through the same program. This is one of Carlson's most important contributions that is not fully implemented in state, county, or private corrections.

Architectural Design

Facing the fact that population growth in the 1970s and beyond would require several new correctional institutions, Norman Carlson became committed to the construction of facilities that expressed his corrections philosophy. He had an architect and a planning committee with wide experience who understood that Carlson wanted institutions in which the form or design followed the function or intended purpose of the facility. As a result, the prisons built by the Federal Bureau of Prisons, especially under Carlson's watch, had meaningful designs. Unfortunately, many prisons built in the United States in the past twenty years lack any sort of meaningful design. With so many, their form in no way corresponds or follows their function.

Development of Leadership

One of the main reasons that Carlson's leadership was so effective was his uncanny ability to identify the potential in individuals. When he saw the potential for leadership in individuals, he knew that with education, training, and motivation, they could develop and contribute to the vision of what he saw for the Bureau of Prisons. He was aware that his task was to provide tools to help them grow and become top-notch corrections employees. Accordingly, he developed the resources for these individuals to realize their potential.

Beginning with those in whom he saw potential, he provided the structure and framework for the potential transformation, both of the system and the individual. Those who responded and grew with corresponding positive career moves expressed gratitude and loyalty to their leader. They felt that their leader was the best; they saw themselves as playing a valued role on the team, and they perceived the Bureau to be an outstanding agency.

Unquestionably, Norman Carlson was able to develop leadership into an art form. Much of the enthusiasm of those who benefitted from his leadership occurred because of how his leadership manifested itself in their lives. This is part of the reason the interviewees, most of whom had experienced their growth as leaders, were so positive about the Director. In all of corrections today, there is a need for those gifted in leadership development to step forth and become, as Carlson was, a positive force for change and growth in their agencies.

Conclusions

One must be very cautious not to generalize too much, because correctional leaders in non-federal agencies across the nation have many of these traits. Still, some correctional agencies would profit from developing these positive characteristics of Carlson's leadership. Some are more important than others, especially clarity of mission, removal of the dichotomy between custody and treatment, and the ability to recognize and develop leadership.

Endnotes

1. Peter Bensinger, former Director of the Drug Enforcement Administration (DEA), was interviewed December 2005.

2. Gordon H. Faulkner was interviewed October 1978.

Chapter 14

Summary

John DiIulio, Jr., one of the most widely recognized critics of correctional administration, sent the author this letter evaluating the quality of Norman A. Carlson as a correctional leader and a public servant:

> Norm Carlson was not only a model corrections leader, he was a model public leader and manager. The special leadership and management challenges he faced concerned not only institutional corrections as such, but also trying to keep a handle on a far-flung federal bureaucracy subject to all manner of political and legal constraints. But whether walking the prison corridors or testifying in Congress, whether coping with some crisis or handling the daily grind, Carlson found a way to lead.
>
> During his tenure, he not only protected the agency from the usual vulnerabilities to mismanagement and corruption, but he opened the agency to new ideas about how to affect old missions. He not only reinforced the agency's strong in-group culture, but also somehow managed to get the wardens and other managers to reach beyond the walls to communities, to the press and to interested academics. He not only forged good relations with his shifting Justice superiors and attorneys general—one of whom became one of his agency's "customers"—but he also managed to defend the agency's best practices in courts of law and in the court of public opinion.

I studied Carlson's leadership up close some two decades ago now. In retrospect and given the subsequent work I did on the federal bureaucracy more generally via the Brookings Institution in the mid-1990s, his leadership and management prowess only looks all the greater—and it looked pretty darn good to me back then.

Above all, Carlson has never been afraid to advocate whatever his best professional understanding of an issue tells him is the truth, or the best alternative, or the least bad option. Sometimes he sounded progressive, sometimes conservative, but always honest and "firm but fair." To me, he remains one of the most accomplished top federal government administrators, without regard to field, of the latter half of the 20th century.[1]

A theme of this biography is that Norman Carlson's positive leadership was instrumental in forging change in federal, state, county, and private corrections agencies. Professor John DiIulio, Jr. certainly articulates this theme in his letter. Yet, in addition to Carlson, the progress in corrections in recent years has come from a number of remarkable prison wardens as well as top executives of corrections agencies.

This biography contains many statements by interviewees in various levels of government, including Congress, Attorneys General, Associate and Assistant Attorneys General, and federal judges, expressing their thoughts.

In the Senate on August 20, 1982, Senator Fritz Hollings presented a tribute to Norm as an outstanding correctional professional and his remarks are part of the *Congressional Record*. Senator Hollings explained that he had worked with Norm for more than ten years, as they had been associated with the U.S. Senate Appropriations Subcommittee on Commerce, Justice, Science and Related Agencies. Of the hundreds of witnesses who testified before his committee, none had impressed him more than the [then] present Director of the

Bureau of Prisons. Senator Hollings stated:

> [Carlson's] presentations to the subcommittee are a model of succinctness and clarity that should be a model for all witnesses before the Appropriations Committee. During his brief annual visits to the committee, we can sense the warmth of this giant of a man and know that firm compassion is the watchword of the Federal prison system. Those who know the inner working of the Bureau of Prisons realize that it is much like a large family. That good atmosphere is maintained by the Director who travels extensively to all the facilities, rises early in the morning to eat breakfast with the inmates, and seems to know all of the employees as he walks through the facilities to assure his standards of care.[2]

Senator Hollings noted that Norm was named a delegate to the United Nations Committee on Crime Prevention and Control in 1971, was co-chairman of the 1975 U.S. delegation to the United Nations Congress on Prevention of Crime and Treatment of Offenders held in Geneva, and was co-chairman of a similar delegation in 1980 in Caracas, Venezuela.[3]

Senator Hollings also mentioned that Norman Carlson served as an advisor to the College of Public and International Affairs of the American University, Washington, D.C., was a member of the Harvard Law School Advisory Committee of the Center for Criminal Justice, was part of the visiting committee of the School of Criminal Justice, State University of New York at Albany, and on the University of Maryland Advisory Board of the Institute of Criminal Justice and Criminology.[4]

The final sections of this summary examine two questions: What made Norman A. Carlson an outstanding corrections professional and what does the example of his leadership offer the wider society?

What made Norman A. Carlson an Outstanding Corrections Professional?

One central argument of this book is that Norman Carlson's leadership moved the Bureau of Prisons from a standard-setting agency to an even better agency. We have discussed his management principles (Chapter 8), his innovations (Chapter 9), and the ripples of his leadership (Chapter 10), but we need to move the analysis of his leadership to the next level. What are the underlying traits of his leadership?

- Norm lived at a level of continuous integrity and expected that staff members of the Bureau of Prisons would also perform at this level. He wanted to maintain the highest possible standards in his own life, and the highest personal standards in government.
- He was committed to excellence and was resolved to do everything possible to achieve it. Nearly all of the interviewees stated that Norman Carlson not only expected excellence he demanded it. This pursuit of excellence became the theme of his career, and it did create some anxiety among employees, especially those in the Bureau's correctional institutions.
- He pursued a learning or growth, model. He was always seeking to grow, to improve the Bureau, and to find new ways of positively challenging staff. This process model contributed to the Bureau becoming a better agency in a number of ways.
- He was proactive in his approach. Norman Carlson pursued a philosophy of anticipating problems before they erupted into institutional chaos. He was aware of the consequences of crisis-centered management around him. With his intuitive ability to see what was coming around the corner, he always tried to stay ahead of institutional and agencywide problems. His approach was anticipatory and preventative.
- He knew where he wanted to take the Bureau and by what specific means and that vision was clearly communicated throughout the Bureau. One interviewee said that "every employee I have known from Alcatraz to Marion and Florence, Colorado

was proud that the Bureau set the standards for American corrections and that they were part of that process."[5]
- He was able to develop the potential in individuals, and was able to provide tools and encouragements to help them grow and become top-notch corrections employees.
- He was able bring all this together in a culture in which the vast majority of staff had amazing loyalty to the Bureau and commitment to Carlson's vision.

Vision for the Wider Society

What do we need to do to transform our society? Perhaps we need to become part of groups to renew our values, to raise our consciousness, or to shake off the shackles of materialism and narcissism. When these newly constituted groups become a critical mass, then sweeping societal change would take place.

Certainly, such groups committed to the environment, to alternative means of medicine, or to economic sufficiency and well-being have influenced systemwide awareness and sometimes caused change. For example, consider our awareness and commitment to the environment that we had thirty years or more ago, and realize what significant leaps we have made.

Still, the vision of society that Gardner articulated in two books nearly fifty years ago has not been attained. Gardner's books are "concerned with the important business of toning up a whole society, of bringing a whole people to that fine edge of morale and conviction and zest that makes for greatness." Nearly no one is satisfied with society as it is. Both from the radical left and from the reactionary right, from the athiests to the arch-religious conservative, from those who have given up on society to those who are passionately pushing their visions for realizing change, there is widespread criticism of where things are. Today, as rarely found in our nation's history, how we get from here to there remains a mystery, a conundrum, a puzzle beyond the best minds and "think tanks." Perhaps, even worse, there is the widespread belief that fundamental change in society will not happen and that we are stuck in the way things have been in the past.

Perhaps the most noteworthy aspect to Norman A. Carlson's life is not that he was a outstanding leader, which he was, not that he contributed in so many ways toward the Bureau of Prisons becoming an even more excellent agency, which he did, but in what his visions offers to society today.

Norm Carlson's qualities represented the very best characteristics found in the history of this nation. Those who worked for Norm used words such as "it was my honor," "he represented greatness," "he embodies quality in everything he does," "those on the Hill thinks he walks on water," "he was a hard worker," and "what he says to you, you can take to the bank."

What comes to mind ultimately is a Midwesterner who went to a small religious college and who worked his way up to the head of the Bureau of Prisons. He never lost his authenticity. He never forgot what it meant to be grounded. He brought to our attention the best of the past and the hope for our future.

Norman Carlson is a reminder to those considering corrections as a career or who are early in their corrections careers of what it is possible for them to accomplish. Ultimately, Norman Carlson's life and leadership is a reminder that humans can be more than they usually are, that there is far more to human potential than we can see in our clearest moments, and that humans joined together with others of kindred minds and spirits can transform the earth. John Gardner's books add to the possibility of human potential, a vision of effecting change and renewal in society. When we raise our sights, strive for excellence, dedicate ourselves to the highest goals of our society, we are enrolling in an ancient and meaningful cause—the age long struggle of humans to realize the best that is in them.

Endnotes

1. John Dilulio, Jr. sent the author a letter on January 17, 2006.

2. Ibid.

3. *Congressional Record: Proceedings and Debates of the 97th Congress, Second Session*, Vol. 128, Washington, D.C., Thursday, August 20, 1982.

4. Ibid.

5. *Steve Grzegorek* was interviewed August 2005.

6. John W. Gardner. 1984/1961. *Can We be Equal and Excellent Too? Revised Edition.* New York: W. W. Norton and Co., p. 11.

Index

A

ACA. *See* American Correctional Association
Academic criminologists, 144
Accountability, 198
Accreditation. *See* Standards and Accreditation of the American Correctional Association
Administrators, high turnover of, 46. *See also* Professional management of administrators
Advisory Corrections Council, 158
Affirmative action, xiv, 48-49
African Americans, 48, 76; first warden (Lee Jett), 133-134; impact of incarceration on, 179; Pat Sledge (dedication to), x-xi; racial integration in Federal Bureau of Prisons, 132-135
AIDS, 120, 121
Alabama correctional system, 181
Alaska Department of Corrections, 137
Alcatraz, 25, 158, 171-174, 178, 195
Alcatraz: The Gangster Years (Ward), 174
Alcoholics Anonymous (AA), 20-21
Alderson (West Virginia) women's prison, 29
Alexander, Myrl E., 5, 24, 27, 34, 41; "Bill of Rights for the Person under Restraint in a Free Democratic Society," 32-33; Carlson as executive assistant to, v, 17, 26, 43; internships, 169; retirement of, 26; as third director of Federal Bureau of Prisons, 32-33; youth facility in Morgantown, West Virginia, vi
Alexander, Will, 79-80
Alternatives to imprisonment, 195
American Academy of Psychiatry and the Law, 56
American Civil Liberties Union, National Prison Project, 51, 110, 181-182
American Correctional Association (ACA); Alexander as president of, 32; annual Congresses of Corrections, 85; Carlson as president of, 150, 153; Carlson's history with, ix, 3; meetings of, 198; Past President's Council, 76; presidential address by Carlson (1980), 56; standards and accreditation process of, ix, 152, 194-195; *Standards Supplement of 2010*, ix
American Penal System as a Revolutionary Target (national symposium), 50
American Prison System, The (Haynes), 19
American University (D.C.), College of Public and International Affairs, 211
Anderson, Eric, 181-182
Architectural design of prisons, 137-140, 206
Arizona Department of Corrections, 193
Arizona State Prison, 193
Arkansas correctional system, 181, 194

Aryan Brotherhood gang, 124, 193
Ashland (Kentucky) Federal Correctional Institution, v, 24-25, 35
Atlanta Penitentiary, 28, 52; Cuban prisoners in, 68, 121-122; gang murders at, 124-125; staff training at, 131-132
Attica State Prison, 132; riot at, 47, 51, 59
Attorney General's office, 8, 128, 147, 160-162, 210
Atwood, Alan, 18
Augustana Lutheran Church, 14
Aun, Michael, 53

B

Babbit, George, 193
Bagdikian, Ben H., *Caged: Eight Prisoners and Their Keepers*, 54-55
Balanced Model of corrections, 56, 191
Barboza, "The Animal," 164
Barkin, Eugene, 99, 141
Bartollas, Clemens, ix, 178-179; about the author, 233; *Becoming a Model Warden: Striving for Excellence*, xiii
Bates, Sanford, 24, 27, 34, 41; first director of Federal Bureau of Prisons, 30; *Prisons and Beyond*, 30
Becoming a Model Warden: Striving for Excellence (Bartollas), xiii
Bell, Griffin, 153, 163, 199
Bennett, James V., 5, 24, 27, 34, 41; and Alcatraz, 173, 195; and Carlson, 25; and Chief Justice Burger, 67; inmate classification system, 31; internships, 169; large desk of, 92; military style of, 44; and professional bureaucracy, 195; and professionalization of Federal Bureau of Prisons, 128, 198; retirement of, 25-26; as second director of Federal Bureau of Prisons, 30-32; and Sentencing Institutes, 150; weapons out of prisons, 139; Youth Corrections Act, 24
Bensinger, Peter, 158-159, 203
"Bill of Rights for the Person under Restraint in a Free Democratic Society" (Alexander), 32-33
Black gangs, 124, 193
Black Guerilla Army, 193
Blackman, Harry, 71
Blackwell, Olin, 42
Board of Parole, 29
Breed, Allen, 173
Bribes, 70, 121
Bronstein, Alvin J., 51, 55, 110, 181 182, 198
Brookings Institute, 210
Brooklyn Federal Detention Center, 171
Brown, Mary, 113
Brutality, 30, 194
Bruton, Jim, 195
Brutsche, Robert, 43-44, 103, 159 160
Bureau of Prisons, 177-186; archives of, 9; as career agency versus political agency, 115; censorship, 53; clearinghouse for information and statistics, 346 *(see also* National Institute of Corrections); core values of, vi, vii; corruption in, 70; culture of, 8; directors of, v, 4, 24, 27 (photograph), 98, 191; establishment of, 29; evaluation by correctional expert, 182-186; excellence of, 23 24; executive staff development, 192; family culture of, 184-185,

209; federal court intervention on inmates' rights, 180-181; good leadership continuity, 185; from a good to a great organization, 149, 177, 212; high recidivism rates, 178; institutional impact on inmates, 178-179; Institutional Programs Division, v; Internal Affairs Unit, 144-145; international comparisons of U.S. prisons, 181-182; merit not patronage, 33; minority hiring, 47-48, 51; mission statement of, vi, viii, 6, 8; as model for state systems, 109; Office of Internal Affairs, 201; policy driven organization, 189; positive organizational culture, 116; psychiatric hospital for, 71-72; quality of life of inmates and staff, 179-180; reasons for outstanding management, 185; rehabilitation concepts of, 55-57; relationships with other agencies, 9; shortcomings of prisons or correctional systems, 177; statistics on, v; support to states, 196; transfers of inmates, 196; uniform disciplinary process, 185; *see also* History of the Federal Bureau of Prisons; Innovations and change; Management; Prison industries

Bureaucratic structure, reducing, vi

Bureau of Efficiency, 30

Burger, Warren E., 54, 63, 67, 71

Butner Federal Correctional Institution, 181-185; experiment at, 143-144; Levinson additions to Morris' model, 144; media reactions, 144; Morris' model, 143; national behavioral research center, 48; program evaluation, 144; Research Triangle evaluation, 144; self-help programs, 143; voluntary participation, 144

Byrd, Mary Leftridge, 195

C

Caged: Eight Prisoners and Their Keepers (Bagdikian), 54-55

Caldwell, Robert G., mentoring students, 16-18

California Department of Corrections, 128, 195, 198

California Department of Penology, 30

Callison, Jack B., 65

Canada, assistance to corrections in, 151-152

Carlson, Albert (father), 14, 75

Carlson, Cindy (daughter), 14, 75, 170

Carlson, Esther (mother), 14, 75

Carlson, Gary (son), 14, 75, 77, 170

Carlson, Lavonne (sister), 14, 75

Carlson, Norman A.; advisory and public service activities, 211; and American Correctional Association (ACA), ix, 3; areas of achievements, 8; authorized biography of, ix Blue Ridge Mountains cabin, 171; career with the Federal Bureau of Prisons, v, xiv, 7, 21; college years and graduate school, 16-20; *Corrections in the 21st Century* (with Karen Hess and Christine Orthman), 85; early life, 13-16; endorsements from staff, 3-7; fast rise to the top, 23-37; as fourth director of Federal Bureau of Prisons, 35, 40; Gardner's influence on, 1-3; interviews and scrapbooks, 9; Iowa Department of Corrections, 13, 20-21; problems as new director of Federal Bureau of Prisons, 114;

religious convictions of, 95-96;
retirement, xiv, 40; swearing in as
Director of the Bureau of Prisons,
27; work at Iowa State Penitentiary,
17-20; *see also* Carlson's influence
and contributions to corrections;
Director of Federal Bureau of
Prisons (1980s); Director of
Federal of Prisons (1970s);
Personal attributes;
Post-retirement years
Carlson, Pat Musser (first wife), 14,
16, 21, 25, 75, 77, 96, 101
Carlson, Phyllis (second wife), 14,
76
Carlson's influence and contributions
to corrections, 189-215; architectural design, 206; *Congressional
Record*, 210-211; corruption-free
operations, 201, 209; custody and
treatment dichotomy, 205; Federal
Bureau of Prisons, 189-191, 209;
leadership development, 206-207;
leadership style, 114-117;
letter evaluating Carlson as a
correctional leader and public
servant, 209-210; paradigm shift,
203-204; partisan issues (political
patronage), 193, 204-205;
proactive leadership, 200
professionalization of staff, 190,
198-199; standards and accreditation
of the American Correctional
Association, 199 200; state
correctional systems, 192-196;
traits of Carlson's leadership, 189,
212-213; vision for wider society,
213-214; see also Personal
attributes; Professional
management of administrators
Carter, Jimmy, 121-122, 162, 163
Casework supervisor, Carlson as, 25
Castro, Fidel, 63, 121

Censorship, 53-55
Centers for Disease Control, 121
Chamlee, Don, 172
Change in Society, xv, 213-214
Chicago Metropolitan Correctional
Center, 165
Childers, Allen, 41
Chillicothe (Ohio) reformatory, 29
Church of the New Song, 52-53;
federal court intervention on
inmates' rights, 180-181; inmate
interviews with the press, 54-55;
inmates publishing, 53
Civil rights, xiv
Civil Service regulations, 30
Civil War, 90
Civiletti, Benjamin, 6, 124, 153-154,
161, 199
Clark, John, x-xi
Classification system for inmates
(SENTRY), 31, 118-119, 190-191
Cleanliness of person, 32, 96, 112,
185
Clutts, Merle Eugene, 64
Coleman (Florida) Federal
Correctional Institution, 171
College of Public and International
Affairs, American University
(D.C.), 211
Collins, Jim, 177
Colson, Charles W., 167-169; *Life
Sentence*, 167, 168
Committee on Administration and
Probation Systems, 158
Common Cause, 1
Community corrections, 31, 35, 48,
191
Community Treatment Centers
Carlson working in, v; halfway
houses, 25
Community Treatment Program, 55
Computers in prison management, vi
Congressional Record, 50, 210-211

Connecticut Department of Corrections, 128, 193, 197, 198
Connolly, Ruth Westrick, 6-7, 8, 71-72
Conrad, John, 44
Constitutional issues, xiv, 51-55;
Coolidge, Calvin, 30
Cooper Commission, 31
Core values of Federal Bureau of Prisons, vi, vii
Corrections in the 21st Century (Carlson, Hess, and Orthman), 85
Corruption in Federal Bureau of Prisons, 70; corruption-free operations, 200-201, 209; Terminal Island, 63, 70
Cost efficiencies, vi, vii
Country club prisons, 111
Court order, prisons under, 181
Criminal Division, Department of Justice, 5
Criminal Law Subcommittee, U.S. Senate Judiciary Committee, 66
Cripe, Clair, 141
Cuban prisoners, 68, 121-122, 192
Culture of Federal Bureau of Prisons, 8, 116; family culture of, 184 185, 209
Cumberland (MD) Federal Correctional Institution, 171
Custody and treatment dichotomy, 47, 114, 130-131, 205

D

Danbury (Connecticut) Federal Correctional Institution, 122
Dark Ages of Corrections. *See* State correctional systems
Davis, Blake, 3-4, 171
Davis, Melvin Lee (Muhammad Abdul Malik), 69
Day, Sherman, 4-5, 93, 95, 131-132, 163

DEA. See Drug Enforcement Administration
Death penalty; for federal crimes, 65-67
Decentralizing authority in prisons, 137
Delaware Department of Corrections, 33
Denmark, 181
Department of Criminology, Indiana State University, 19
Detail, attention to, 197
DiIulio, John, Jr., 113, 182-185, 198, 209-210
Dinitz, Simon, 178-179
Direct supervision of inmates, 191; *see also* Unit manangement
Director of Federal Bureau of Prisons (1970s), 39-61; appointment of, 40-41; boredom of inmates, 45; challenges of correctional administration, 44 47; changing role of rehabilitation, 55-57; conflict between custody and treatment staff, 47; *Congressional Record* comment, 50; and crowding, 58-59; First National Conference on Corrections, 47-49; high turnover of administrators, 46; homosexual activity, 49; "house boys," 43; inmate rights, 46, 51-55; Lake Placid prison, 57-58; legal aspects of corrections management, 51-55; letter to Bureau staff on his appointment as Director, 41-42; Lewisburg Penitentiary violence, 47, 49-50, 51; militancy, 42; officers' messes, 43; outside agitators, 47, 50-51; political nature of corrections, 46; politicization of inmates, 50-51; prison population numbers, 42,

44-45, 48, 58-59; prison reform and prison violence, 47-49; prison violence, 45, 47-50; racial conflict, 45, 48; staff violence, 45; suicide incidents, 45; ten-year plan, 42; unit management, 49-50, 94; visits to BOP prisons, 51; Wardens' Conference, 42, 43

Director of Federal Bureau of Prisons (1980s), 63-74; Carlson's statement on death penalty for killing federal officers, 66-67; corrupt correctional officers at Terminal Island, 63, 70; final eight years as director, 63; incarceration of deported Cubans, 68; inmate jobs, 67-68; psychiatric hospital for the Bureau of Prisons, 71-72; shooting at the homes of Carlson and his assisstant, 69; violence at Marion (Illinois) Penitentiary, 63, 64-67;

Disciplinary process, uniform, 185

Disciplinary process in Bureau of Prisons, 185

Discipline in state prisons, 194

Ditterline, Roger D., 64, 65

Dress code for staff members, 130

Drug Enforcement Administration (DEA), 203

Drugs, selling in prisons, xiv, 70

Duvall v. Schaefer, 84

E

Earley, Pete, 129-130, 159

Eclatarian Bible, 52

Edenfield, Newell, 52-53

Educational programs for inmates, 48, 194

EEO. See Equal Employment Opportunity

El Reno (Oklahoma) Federal Correctional Institution, 35, 132, 133

Elderly inmates' medical concerns, 120

Emergency Response Squad (SWAT team), 24

Engel, Richard, 171

Englewood (Colorado) Federal Correctional Institution, 24, 25, 35, 171

Equal Employment Opportunity (EEO), gender and racial integration in Federal Bureau of Prisons, 132-135

Excellence, commitment to, 43, 90, 93-94, 111, 185, 212

F

Family culture of Bureau of Prisons, 113, 184-185, 211

Farkas, Jerry, 121, 122

Faulkner, Gordon H., 204

FBI, 121, 129, 145, 172

Federal Bureau of Prisons. *See* Bureau of Prisons

Federal Criminal Justice System, 66

Federal judges, 155-158, 210

Federal Judicial Center, 156

Federal judiciary, 8

Federal Medical Center in Springfield, Missouri, x, 140-141

Federal Medical Clinic in Rochester, Minnesota, 6, 171

Federal Prison Industries. See Unicor

Federal probation, 172

Federal probation law, 29

Federal Witness Protection Programs (WITSEC), 5, 149, 164-167

Female health issues, 120

Fenton, Charles, 50

Fire Prevention, 122

First Amendment, 51, 52

First National Conference on
Corrections, 47-49
Florence (CO) Federal Maximum
Security Penitentiary, 173
Folsom prison riots, 51
Food, improvement in, 194
Ford, Gerald, 57-58
Fort Madison, Iowa State
Penitentiary, 17 20
Fort Worth Federal Correctional
Institution, 146
Fountain, Clayton, 64
Fratianno, Aladena "Jimmy the
Weasel," 164
Future of Imprisonment, The
(Morris), 48, 55, 143

G

Gaines, Russell, 100
Gangs in prisons, xiv, 119, 120-121,
124-125, 150, 193
Gardner, John W., 1-3, 7, 8, 213, 214;
*Excellence: Can We Be Equal and
Excellent Too?*, 1, 2
*Self-Renewal: The Individual and
the Innovative Society*, 1, 2
Gender and racial integration in
Federal Bureau of Prisons, Equal
Employment Opportunity (EEO),
132-135
GEO Group, Inc., 3; Carlson on
board of directors of, 76, 85
Georgia Department of Corrections,
193
Georgia State University, 4, 131
Gerard, Roy, 63, 92, 94, 136
Gesell, Gerhard A., 4, 55
Giuliani, Rudy, 78
Goffee, Rob and Gareth Jones, *Why
Should Anyone Be Led by You*,
146-147
Gravano, Sammy "The Bull," 164
Great Depression, 30

Grievance process for inmates, 192
Griswold, Erwin N., 54
Grzegorek, Steve, 23, 75, 115-116,
120-121
Gustavus Adolphus, St. Peter,
Minnesota, 15-16, 150, 170-171
Gustavus Quarterly, 170-171

H

Halfway houses, 31; Community
Treatment Centers, 25; Prerelease
Guidance Centers, 35
Hambrick, Margaret, 91-92, 134-135
Hanson, Bill, 15
Harassment, 199
Harvard Law School Advisory
Committee, Center for Criminal
Justice, 211
Hawaii Department of Corrections,
82, 83-84
Hayes, Loy, Jr., 103
Haynes, Frederick E., *American
Prison System, The*, 19
Henderson, G. F., 89
Henderson, James D., 115
Hepatitis B and C, 120
Hess, Karen, 85
High-risk situations, 120-121.
See also Incident management
Hill, Henry, 164
Hiring ex-offenders, 146
Hispanics, gender and racial
integration in Federal Bureau of
Prisons, 132-135
History of the Federal Bureau of
Prisons, 28-35; early history, 28-
29; era of James Bennett, 30-32;
era of Myrl Alexander, 32-33; era
of Sanford Bates, 30; *see also*
Bureau of Prisons; *Prisons and
the American Conscience: A
History of U.S. Federal
Corrections* (Keve)

HIV, 120
Hoffman, Robert L., Sr., 64, 65
Hollings, Senator Fritz, 210-211
Hollingsworth, Lisa Warner, 171
Hoover, Herbert, 29
Hoover, J. Edgar, 25-26, 172
Houk, Wade, 3, 99, 159
Houston Chronicle, 54
Hughes, Senator (Iowa), 167
Humane prison defined, 181-182
Humane treatment of inmates, 8, 117-120; Bates on, 30; Butner (NC) Federal Correctional Institution, 182-185; and Carlson, 6-7, 51; classification (SENTRY), 118-119; decency and respect, 117; and gang activities, 119; inmate grievance system, 140-141; as individuals, 33; lock-downs, 119; medical and dental services, 120; opportunities for individual growth, 119; privacy, 118; programs for, 84; racial tensions, 119; recreational services, 120; rehabilitation, 56; rights and privileges of inmates, 110, 113; safety of inmates, 117-118; safety of staff, 110, 118; see also Inmates; Management and principles of leadership
Humphrey Institute of Public Affairs, University of Minnesota, 76, 77, 81
Humphrey, Michelle, 4, 100
Hunt, Elayn, 195
Hunt, Teresa, 171
Hurley, John, 99, 109, 116-117

I

Iannuzzi, Joseph "Joe Dogs," 164
Illinois Department of Corrections, 84, 203

Incident management, 120-125; AIDS in prison, 121; Cubans in prison, 121-122; essence of issues in simple terms, 123-124; fire at Danbury, 122; high-risk situations, 120-121; murders at Atlanta, 124-125; see also Management
Indiana State University, Department of Criminology, 19
Individualized treatment programs, 31
Industries. *See* Prison industries
Infectious diseases, 120
Ingram, Gil, 91, 102, 142
Inmates, abuse of, xiv; boredom of, 45; and censorship, 53; civil rights of, xiv; classification system for (SENTRY), vi-vii, 31, 118-119, 190-191; communication with, vii; community adjustment of, 178; direct supervision of, 191; drug and alcohol abuse, 178; educational programs for, 194; elderly inmates' medical concerns, 120; and family lies, 32; grievance process for, 192; growth in population, viii, xiv; growth of individuals, 119; homosexual activity of, 49; "house boys," 43; humane treatment of, xiv, 6, 8, 33, 34, 117; individualized attention for, vi; as individuals, 34; institutional impact on, 178-179; Jaycees chapter for, 25; jobs for, 67-68; labor of, 194; memoirs of, 180; movement of, 198; politicization of, 50-51; population in facilities of Bureau of Prisons, v; privacy of, 118; publications of, 53-55; quality of life of, 179-180; racial conflict, 40, 45, 48; respect for, vi, xiv, 7; rights of, 46, 51-55,

192; safety of, 117-118; skills development for, vi, vii-viii; suicide incidents, 45; transfers of, 151, 152, 196; vocational and educational programs for, 194; *see also* Constitutional issues; Gangs in prisons; Humane treatment of inmates

Innovations and change, 127-148; architectural design, 137-140, 206; Carlson's biggest accomplishment, 129-130; co-corrections facilities, 146; decentralizing authority in the institution, 137; effective change agent, 127-128; experiment at the Butner Federal Correctional Institution, 143-144; Federal Bureau of Prisons as a family, 142; first woman warden's career, 134-135; gender and racial integration, 132-135; hiring ex-offenders, 146; inmate grievance system, 140-141; Office of Internal Affairs established, 144-145; professionalization of the agency, 128-132, 137; regionalization, 135-136; staff training, 130-132; systematic pursuit of, 2; unit management, 136-137;

Institutional Programs Division, v

Integrity, vi, xiv, 212

International comparisons of U.S. prisons, 181-182

International Transfer of Offenders, 152

Internship program, 169-171

Iowa State Penitentiary, Fort Madison, 17-20

Iranian demonstrators, 69

J

Jabobs, James, 113
Jackson, Stonewall, 89, 90
Jacobs, James, 198
Jaycees chapter for inmates, 25
Jelinek, David, 135-136, 142, 158
Jett, Lee, 133-134, 137
Jordan, Hamilton, 163
Juvenile correctional institutions, 179

K

Kennedy, Robert F., 6, 25, 35, 100
Kent State University, 150, 169, 170
Keohane, Patrick, 91, 94, 98
Keve, Paul W., *Prisons and the American Conscience: A History of U.S. Federal Corrections*, 33-35
Kirschbaum, Ira, 141

L

La Cosa Nostra (LCN), 164
Lainson, Percy, 18, 20, 21
Laird, Paul, 170 171
Lake Placid, Winter Olympics (1980), 57-58
Lappin, Harley, 170, 190-191, 201; Foreword by, v-viii
Latino Americans, 48
Law Enforcement Assistance Administration (LEAA), 48, 49, 154
LEAA. *See* Law Enforcement Assistance Administration
Leadership, 209-210; continuity of, 185; development of, 206-207; proactive, 114, 200-201; traits of, 27, 90-91, 104, 189, 212-213
Leavenworth, Kansas, U.S. Penitentiary, v, 21, 23, 24, 28, 129
Legal Aid Society, 82

Legal aspects of corrections management, 51-55
Legal changes relating to corrections, 185
Levinson, Robert, 94-95, 96, 127, 136, 144
Lewisburg Federal Correctional Institution, violence at, 47, 49-50, 51, 102
Lexingtion Federal Correctional Institution, 146
Life Magazine, 13, 200
Life Sentence (Colson), 167
Lockdowns, 119
Long Beach State University, 154
Lorton Reformatory, 41
Louisiana corrections, 195
Lucas, Malcolm M., 70
Lyles, Dick, 133

M

MacDougall, Ellis C., 162-163, 192-196
Mafia, 164
Magnuson, Paul, 155-156
Malik, Muhammad Abdul (Davis, Melvin Lee), 69
Management, xiv, 109-126, 149, 184-185; leadership style, 110, 114-115; management principles, 111-114; participatory management, 115-117; positive organizational culture, 116; shift in leadership style, 115-117; *see also* Humane treatment of inmates; Incident management
"Management by walking around" (MBWA), 43, 112, 183, 197
Mariel boatlift of 1980, 68, 192
Marijuana, selling to inmates, 70
Marion (IL) United States Penitentiary, 63-67, 94, 171-174, 180, 195

Martin, Steve J., 82-84, 109
Martinson, Floyd, 16
Martinson, Robert, "What Works?: Questions and Answers About Prison Reform," 55
Maryland Department of Corrections, 84
Massoglia, Michael, 77, 80-81, 179
Matthews, Bob, 101, 129, 132
Mayo Clinic, 71
MBWA. See "Management by walking around"
McCorkle, Lloyd, 195
McEwen, Robert C., 57-58
McGee, Richard A., 195
McNeil Island, Washington, 28
Medical care, 29, 120
Medical model in criminology, vii, 55, 56, 191
Meese, Edwin, 6, 40, 160
Meko, James A., 69, 100
Menninger Clinic, 137, 155
Menninger, Walter, 113, 137-138, 155, 198
Mental health problems, 120
Mentoring, 113
Metropolitan Correctional Centers, 191-192
Mexican gangs, 124
Mexican Mafia, 193
Michigan Department of Corrections, 84
Militancy, 42
Miller, Stuart J., 178-179
Minnesota Community Corrections Act, 195
Minnesota Correctional Facilities at Stillwater and Oak Park Heights, 117, 200
Minnesota Department of Corrections, 81, 128, 195, 197, 198
Minnesota State Hospital, 71

Minorities, gender and racial integration in Federal Bureau of Prisons, 132-135; hiring, 47-48, 51. *See also* Affirmative Action; African Americans; Latino Americans
Mission clarity, 197
Mission statement of Federal Bureau of Prisons, vi, viii, 6, 8
Mississippi Department of Corrections, 193, 194
Mississippi State Prison (Parchment), 193
Mitchell, John N., 17, 26, 40, 48, 102, 111, 160
Mitchell, William DeWitt, 29
Model for state systems, 109, 150, 195, 209
Moeller, Gus, 41, 42
Morgantown Federal Correctional Institution, 146, 195
Morgantown, West Virginia, 35
Morris, Norval, 113, 154, 198; *Future of Imprisonment, The*, 48, 55, 143
Mote, Gary R., 69, 95-96, 97, 98, 102, 137, 138-139
Munich Summer Olympics (1972), 57
Munson, Mark, 171
Musser, Pat, 16. *See also* Carlson, Pat

N

Nardini, William, 18, 19
National Archives, 172
National Clearinghouse for Criminal Justice Architecture, University of Illinois, 48
National Institute of Corrections, 154-155, 198; Advisory Board, 76, 84; staff training center, 48
National Institute of Justice, grant for Alcatraz study, 172
National Prison Project, American Civil Liberties Union, 51, 110
National Training School for Boys, Washington, D.C., 35
National Urban Coalition, 1
New Mexico State Prison riot, 51
New York City Federal Metropolitan Correctional Center, 69, 164
New York State University (Albany), School of Criminal Justice, 211
New York Times, 98, 200
Nixon, Richard, 47
"Nothing works" (Martinson), 55

O

Oakdale (Louisiana) Federal Detention Center, and Cuban prisoners, 68
Officers' messes, 43
Ohio Department of Corrections, 195
Organized crime inmates, 120-121, 124-125
Orthman, Christine, 85
Otisville (NY) Federal Correctional Institution, 69
Outside agitators, 47, 50-51
Oxford (WI) Federal Correctional Institution, 171

P

Palmer Prison (Alaska), 137
Paradigm shifts in Norman Carlson's leadership, xiv, 7-9, 149-176; accreditation standards of the American Correctional Association, 152-154; Attorney General's office, 160-162; Federal Bureau of Prisons as a career agency, 162-163; Federal Witness Protection Programs (WITSEC), 149, 164-167; internship program,

169-171; National Institute of Corrections (NIC), 154-155; Prison Fellowship movement, 167-169; Sentencing Institutes with federal judges, 155-158; stablizing influence and positive direction on other agencies, 150-152; United States Congress, 158-160; university research, 171-174
Parole officer, Carlson as, v, 24
Parole system, 29
Participatory management, 115-117
Partisan issues (political patronage), 193, 204-205; Federal Bureau of Prisons as career agency versus political body, 115; merit not patronage, 33; political nature of corrections, 46
Patrick, William, 4, 138, 139-140
Pekin (IL) Federal Correctional Institution, 171
Persico, Carmine "The Snake," 121
Personal attributes, v-vi, xiv, 39, 42-44, 89-107; acuity of mind, 97-98, 189; avid reader, 98-99, 113; command presence, 90, 91-92; communication with staff, 112, 115, 185; cool under fire, 102; good physical health, 103-104; height, 42; humility, 90, 92-93; impatience, 90, 104, 116; integrity, 43, 90, 93, 94-95, 112, 116, 149, 189, 212; intelligence of, 97; intuitive nature, 98, 212; Jackson, Stonewall, 89, 90; kind, gentle, and gracious person, 100-101, 113; mentoring staff, 113; order and cleanliness, 96, 112, 185; outstanding leadership, 27, 90-91, 104, 212-213; personal grounding, 95-96; proactive stance, 112, 114, 125, 212; pursuit of excellence, 90, 93-94, 111, 185, 212; remarkable memory, 102-103; "Stormin' Norman," 99; synthesizer, 98; visionary, 97
Personnel selection, 115
Peters, Thomas J. and Robert H. Waterman, Jr., *Search for Excellence, The*, 93
Pleasanton Federal Correctional Institution, 146
Post-retirement years, 75-85; board participation, 84-85, 155, 211; consulting, 82-84; scholarly activities, 85; spokesperson for corrections, 85; students' response to Carlson as teacher, 78-81; university teaching, 76-82
Powell, Jody, 163
Powles, Jerry L., 64, 65
Pownell George, 169-170
Prerelease Guidance Centers, halfway houses, 35
Princeton University, Woodrow Wilson School of Public and International Affairs, v, 36
Prison architectural design, 111, 137-140; form follows function, 138-139, 206
Prison culture, xiv
Prison Fellowship movement, 167-169
Prison industries, 29, 34-35, 67-68; UNICOR (Federal Prison Industries), 31, 34-35, 67-68
Prisoners. See Inmates
Prisons, AIDS in, 120, 121; architectural design of, 137-140, 206; cleanliness of, 130; decentralizing authority in, 137; international comparisons of U.S. prisons, 181-182; men's and women's, 45; population numbers, 42, 44-45, 48, 58-59;

reform and prison violence, 45, 47-49; sexual victimization in, 45; suicide in, 45; unit management, vi, 191
Prisons and Beyond (Bates), 30
Prisons and the American Conscience: A History of U.S. Federal Corrections (Keve), 33-35
Private corrections, 199
Probation system, 29
Professional management of administrators, 196-198; accountability, 198; management by walking around (MBWA), 197; mission clarity, 197; National Institute of Corrections, 198; professional administrators, 197-198; qualifications for administrators, 196; *see also* Carlson's influence and contributions to corrections
Professionalism, vi, vii, 198-199
Psychiatric hospital for the Bureau of Prisons, 64
Public safety, 113

Q
Quinlan, Michael, 98, 102, 191

R
Racial conflicts, xiv, 48
Ragan, Joseph, 197
Rawlings, Mary, 44, 92, 103
Reagan, Ronald, 6
Recidivism, 178, 197
Reckless, Walter, 178
Recreational services, 120
Reentry, viii. *See also* Rehabilitation
Regionalization, 135-136, 191-192
Rehabilitation, vii-viii, 55-57; "Balanced Approach," 56; changing role of, 55-57;
Community Treatment Program, 55; humanizing institutions, 56; Medical Model, 55, 56; "nothing works" (Martinson), 55; *see also* Reentry
Retirement, 40, 44, 75
Rehnquist, Chief Justice, 157
Research in corrections, vi; Carlson developing, vii
Rights of inmates, 192
Rikers Island, Carlson as special master at, 78; Central Punitive Segregation Unit, 82
Riveland, Chase, 195
Rochester (MN) Federal Medical Center, 71-72, 171
Rochester State Hospital, 71-72
Roosevelt, Franklin Delano, 35

S
Safety and security, vi-vii, 8
Safford (AZ) Federal Correctional Institution, 171
Samples, Pat, 101
Samples, Sam, 3, 93, 132, 183
San Diego Metropolitan Correctional Center, 134, 165
San Quentin prison riots, 51, 59, 158
Sandstone (AZ) Federal Correctional Institution, 171
Santos, Michael G., 180
Sawyer, Kathleen Hawk, 191; on Carlson, 39-40, 189-190; director of Federal Bureau of Prisons, 40
Schedules, compliance with, 198
Schoen, Kenneth F., 195
Schwalb, Steve, 75, 102, 123-124, 144-145
Sea, Darrell, 13, 14, 15
Search of Excellence, The (Peters and Waterman), 93
Seiter, Rick, 3, 97, 161-162

Sentencing Institutes with federal judges, 155-158
SENTRY (inmate classification system), 31, 118-119, 190-191
"Shamming," 143
Sheppard, et al. v. Phoenix et al., 82, 83, 84
Shooting at the homes of Carlson and his assisstant, 69
Shur, Gerald, 4-5, 149, 164-167
Silber, Frederick, 52
Singleton, John V., 54, 55
Sioux City, Iowa, 13, 14
Sixty Minutes, 181
Slack, Robert, 58
Sledge, Pat, x-xi, 93, 100
Sociology Department, University of Minnesota, 76, 77
Softball player, Carlson as, 25
Soledad riots, 59
South Carolina Department of Corrections, 193
Southern Illinois University, 26, 32
Springfield (MO) Federal Medical Center, x, 140-141
St. Paul Police foundation, Board of Directors, 84
St. Peter, MN, Gustavus Adolphus, 15-16, 150, 170-171
Staff members, and abuse of inmates, 45; dress code, 130; of Federal Bureau of Prisons, v; loyalty of, 213; merit not patronage, 34; professionalism of, 116; quality of life of, 179-180; recruitment of, 31, 155; as role models for inmates, vii, safety of, 110, 118; titles from "guards" to "correctional officers," vii, 130, training programs for, vii, 31, 48, 115, 130-132, 190, 205 treatment staff versus custodial staff, 130-131; violence of, 45

Standards and accreditation of the American Correctional Association (ACA), ix, 152-153, 194-195, 199-200
State and local agencies, 48
State correctional systems, 8; Carlson's influence on, 192-196; Federal Bureau of Prisons as model for, 34, 109, 150, 195; LEAA grants to, 49; state correctional leaders, 195; support by Federal Bureau of Prisons, 196
State-Justice-Commerce Appropriations Subcommittee, 210-211
Stone, Harlan F., 29
Stoneman, Kenneth, 195
Story, Bill, 92, 98, 99
Summer Olympics (1972), Munich, 57
Superintendent of Prisons, 28, 30
Supermax prisons, 65, 67, 72
SWAT team (Emergency Response Squad), 24

T

Ten-year plan, 42
Teresa, Vincent "Fat Vennie," 164
Terminal Island (CA), Federal Correctional Institution, 145, 167, 200-201; corrupt correctional officers at Terminal Island, 63, 70
Texas correctional system, 181, 197
Theriault, Harry W., 52-53
Three Prisons Act, 28-29
Tjoflat, Gerald, 156-158, 160
Training. *See* Staff members training programs for
Transfers of inmates, 196
Travisono, Anthony, 150-151, 152-154

Treatment staff versus custodial staff. *See* Custodial and treatment dichotomy
Truman, Harry, 161
Tuberculosis, 120
Turnbo, Charles, 99, 103-104, 133, 142, 146

U

UNICOR (Federal Prison Industries), 31, 33, 34-35, 67-68
Uniform disciplinary process, 185
Unit management, vi, 35, 49-50, 94, 136-137, 184, 191
United Nations, 31; Committee on Crime Prevention and Control, 211; Congress on Crime Prevention, speech by Carlson at, 56-57; and Congress on Prevention of Crime and Treatment of Offenders, 211
United States Bureau of Prisons. *See* Bureau of Prisons
United States Congress, 128, 129, 147, 158-160, 210
United States Constitution. *See* Constitutional issues
United States Department of Justice, 25-26, 28, 79, 129; Criminal Division, 5
United States District Court in Maryland, Carlson as special master, 84
United States District Court, Southern District of New York, Carlson as special monitor for, 84
United States Penitentiary, Leavenworth, Kansas, 21, 23, 24, 28, 129; Marion, Illinois, 63, 94, 171-174, 180, 195
United States Senate Judiciary Committee, Criminal Law Subcommittee, 66
United States Supreme Court, 55
University of California at Berkeley, 76, 172
University of Chicago, 154
University of Chicago Law School, 48
University of Florida, 32
University of Hawaii, 83
University of Illinois, National Clearinghouse for Criminal Justice Architecture, 48
University of Iowa, 16-18
University of Maryland Advisory Board of the Institute of Criminal Justice and Criminology, 211
University of Minnesota, 5; Carlson teaching at, 76-82, Humphrey Institute of Public Affairs, 76, 77, 81
University of Pennsylvania, Wharton School of Business, 154
University of South Carolina, 192
University of Southern California, 154
University research, 171-174
University teaching, 76-82
Utah Department of Corrections, 84

V

Values, consistency of among directors of Federal Bureau of Prisons, 191
Van Duzen, Judge, 156
Velde, Richard "Pete," 154
Vermont, 195
Violence in prisons, xiv
Virginia Commonwealth University, 33
Vision for America, 213-214
Vocational and educational programs for inmates, 194

W

Wall Street Journal, 98
Wallenberg, Al, 158
Ward, David, 5, 76-79, 81, 83, 171, 178; *Alcatraz: The Gangster Years*, 174
Wardens' Conference, 42, 43
Warner, Wendy Roal, 171
Washington Post, 54, 98, 129, 159
Washington state corrections, 195
Watergate, 102, 111
Westrick, Ruth Connolly, 6-7, 71, 72
Wharton School of Business, University of Pennsylvania, 154
"What Works?: Questions and Answers About Prison Reform" (Martinson), 55
White-collar inmates, 111
Why Should Anyone Be Led by You (Goffee and Jones), 146-147
Wilkey, Bill, 154
Wilkinson, George C., 26
Wilkinson, Reginald, 195
Willebrandt, Mabel Walker, 29, 34
Williams, J. D., 133, 134
Williamsburg, VA, First National Conference on Corrections, 47
Williford, Jerry, 65
Wilson, James Q., 113, 182
Winter Olympics (1980), Lake Placid, 57-58
WITSEC. *See* Federal Witness Protection Program
Women, female health issues, 120; first woman warden (Margaret Hambrick), 134-135; gender and racial integration in Federal Bureau of Prisons, 132-135
Wood, Frank, xiii, 7, 117; 195, 200
Woodrow Wilson School of Public and International Affairs at Princeton University, Carlson participation in, v, 36
Worldview, 7. *See also* Paradigm shifts

Y

Yeomans, Don, 151
Youth, 31
Youth Corrections Act, 24

About the Author

Clemens Bartollas is a professor of sociology at the University of Northern Iowa. He holds a B.A. from Davis and Elkins College, a B.D. from Princeton Theological Seminary, an S.T.M. from San Francisco Theological Seminary, and a Ph.D. in sociology, with a special emphasis in criminology, from The Ohio State University. He taught at Pembroke State University from 1973 to 1975, Sangamon State University from 1975 to 1980, and at the University of Northern Iowa from 1981 to the present. He has received a number of honors from the University of Northern Iowa, including Distinguished Scholar, the Donald McKay Research Award, and the Regents' Award for Faculty Excellence.

Professor Bartollas has written forty books, including *Becoming a Model Warden: Striving for Excellence* and *Successful Management of Juvenile Residential Facilities: A Performance-Based Approach*, both of which were published by and are available from the American Correctional Association. Bartollas is probably best known for his works on juvenile institutions, adult prisons, juvenile delinquency, and juvenile corrections. In recent years, Bartollas has also become engaged in studying street gangs, both in the community and in prison contexts.